THE ART OF BALANCING YIN-YANG ENERGY

DISCOVER THE SECRET TO ENERGIZED LIVING; ATTAIN WHOLENESS, FIND INNER EQUILIBRIUM AND SERENITY IN YOUR EVERYDAY EXISTENCE

SOORAJ ACHAR

WWW.SOORAJ-ACHAR.COM

Copyright © 2023 by Sooraj Achar

All rights reserved.

No part of this book may be reproduced in any form without permission in writing from the author.

No part of this publication may be reproduced or transmitted in any form or by any means, mechanical or electronic, including photocopying or recording, or by any information storage and retrieval system, or transmitted by email or by any other means whatsoever without permission in writing from the author.

YOUR FREE GIFT

A s a token of my thanks for taking out time to read my book, I would like to offer you a **Free-Gift**:

Scan Below **QR Code** to Download your **Free eBook PDF**.

Learn 395+ Surprising Psychology Words That Will Change The Way You Think - in the Next 30 Days!

You can also grab your **FREE GIFT** by typing in the below URL: **https://gift.sooraj-achar.com/**

· · · **·** · **·** · · ·

ABOUT AUTHOR

Sooraj Achar, Author of "The Art of Balancing YIN-YANG Energy" - #1_BestSeller in USA, UK, Canada, India & Australia

Mr. Sooraj Achar was born in Bangalore, India. Growing up, he was fascinated with Mathematics, and his interest led to some early exposure to Numbers since he was drawn to stories related to Numerology.

Later, **Sooraj**, who is now a Software Engineer, developed a passion for **Numerology and Feng-Shui (Vastu)**. He is also a **Coach and Consultant**.

Being a Certified **Ho'oponopono & EFT Healer**, **Sooraj** explores the issues of How **Health, Relationships, Careers, & Money (HRCM)** can be Recognized, Transformed, and Navigated **toward a more Balanced, Harmonious, & Fulfilling Life.**

Sooraj loves to research **Human Psychology & Behavior** in order to get the maximum out of life. He is always eager to learn, embody, and then impart the fundamentals of optimal living to help others lead a resourceful life.

He is deeply convinced about the limitlessness of human potential and strongly believes that everyone has the potential to achieve more than one thinks about oneself.

Visit **www.sooraj-achar.com** to know more about his Life-Changing Book Catalogue.

THE ART OF BALANCING YIN-YANG ENERGY

Stay Connected to our below **Social Media Handles**:

https://amzn.to/3CgQHF9

https://medium.com/@soorajachar99

https://bit.ly/3M7gIu2

instagram.com/psychology_of_numberz/

https://bit.ly/3dO6aDh

https://bit.ly/3LXBTyz

https://bit.ly/3E9vKxc

• • • • • • • • •

ACKNOWLEDGEMENTS

How does a person say **"Thank You"** when there are so many people to thank?

Obviously, this book is a big thank you to my father **G Sathyanarayan Achar,** who is a powerful role model, and to my mother **G Pramila,** who taught me love and kindness.

My dearest ones most responsible for this book becoming a reality is my sister **Shruthi S**, brother-in-law **Saravana P,** and my cute niece **Naveeksha S.** They make my life complete.

Special thanks to my Mentor **Mr. Mitesh Khatri**, who taught me and guided me to become a **Ho'Oponopono & EFT - Healer.**

I am grateful to **Mr. Som Bathla**, who is an Amazon **#1 Bestselling** author of multiple books; for mentoring, motivating, and guiding me to Write, Self-Publish, & Launch Books and for helping me start my **Authorpreneur Journey.**

Last but not least, My Team: **Avesh Ansari(Profile), Akshay Bhat(work4ever24h), & Md. Bilal (Iconic_agency).**

• • • • • • • • • •

DEDICATION

This Book is Dedicated to My Grandparents,

R. Gangadharaiah & G. Vishalakshamma

And, My Dear Brother **Arvind Achar.**

• • • • • • • • • •

CONTENTS

How This Book Can Work Miracles In Your Life??	XIII
5 Key Takeaways from Each Chapter	XXII
1. Introduction to Yin-Yang	1
2. Impact of Yin-Yang Frequency	7
3. 3-Steps to Balance Your Energy	22
4. Balance in Different Situations	30
5. Balancing Yin-Yang Energy & Practical Application	46
6. Understanding 7-Energy Chakras	50
7. Sound Meditation for Chakra Activation	67
8. Energy Charging Exercise for 7-Chakras	74

9. Shiva: The Masculine & Feminine Energy Together	83
10. Yin-Yang and Taoism	89
Conclusion	99
May I Ask You for a Small Favor?	100
Preview of My Best Selling Books	103
Testimonials	118
Author Profile	124
Disclaimer	127

How This Book Can Work Miracles In Your Life??

"The Art of Balancing Yin-Yang Energy" is an enlightening and transformative guide that unveils the ancient wisdom of harmonizing the opposing forces of Yin and Yang within ourselves and the world around us. Drawing from the profound teachings of Eastern philosophy and modern-day practices, this book offers a comprehensive understanding of Yin and Yang and provides practical techniques to achieve balance, harmony, and fulfillment in all aspects of life.

In today's fast-paced and chaotic world, finding balance is more crucial than ever. Whether you seek to improve your relationships, enhance your well-being, or achieve success in your career, understanding and aligning the Yin-Yang energy within you can be a game-changer. This book takes you on a transformative journey, guiding you through the principles, practices, and benefits of embracing the art of balancing Yin-Yang energy.

By delving into the core concepts of Yin and Yang, you will gain insights into their dynamic interplay and learn how to identify and rectify imbalances in your life. Discover how the complementary forces of Yin and Yang manifest in various aspects, such as work-life balance, emotional well-being, and personal growth. With this knowledge, you can cultivate harmony and create a fulfilling and purpose-driven life.

"The Art of Balancing Yin-Yang Energy" offers a myriad of practical techniques to help you integrate Yin and Yang into your daily life. From mindfulness exercises to energy healing practices, you will learn how to tap into the transformative power of these forces. Through step-by-step instructions and insightful guidance, you will explore meditation, breathwork, movement, and other modalities that restore equilibrium and vitality.

Unleash the potential of Yin-Yang energy to transform your relationships and deepen your connection with others. Gain valuable insights into the dynamics of partnerships, friendships, and family interactions, and learn how to navigate conflicts and foster harmonious relationships. Discover how to create a nurturing and balanced environment that supports the well-being and growth of everyone involved.

Achieving optimal health and well-being is another significant benefit of balancing Yin and Yang energies. Explore the interplay of Yin-Yang in nutrition, exercise, and self-care routines, and uncover practical tips to restore balance and vitality. Learn how to cultivate mindfulness and listen to your body's needs, enabling you to make conscious choices that promote overall wellness and inner harmony.

Furthermore, "The Art of Balancing Yin-Yang Energy" provides valuable insights for professionals seeking success and fulfillment in their careers. Gain a deeper understanding of work-life balance, stress management, and personal development through the lens of Yin-Yang energy. Discover how to align your passions, values, and skills to create a thriving and purposeful career that brings you joy and satisfaction.

By embracing the wisdom of balancing Yin and Yang, you will experience a profound shift in your life. Unlock your true potential and unleash your creativity, intuition, and inner strength. Witness the transformation as you become more adaptable, resilient, and empowered to navigate life's challenges with grace and wisdom.

In summary, "The Art of Balancing Yin-Yang Energy" is a comprehensive guide that offers a treasure trove of wisdom and practical techniques to cultivate balance, harmony, and fulfillment in all areas of life. Whether you are seeking personal growth, enhanced relationships, improved well-being, or professional success, this book provides the roadmap to unlock the transformative power of Yin-Yang energy. Embrace the ancient art of balance and embark on a journey of self-discovery, empowerment, and transcendence. Your life will never be the same again.

Discover the Ancient Wisdom of Balancing Yin-Yang Energy!

In "The Art of Balancing Yin-Yang Energy," embark on a transformative journey into the depths of Eastern philosophy and holistic wellness. This captivating book unveils the secrets of harmonizing the vital forces of Yin and Yang, creating a profound equilibrium in all aspects of life. From relationships and health to career and spiritual well-being, this guide empowers you to achieve harmony and balance.

Drawing from ancient practices such as Traditional Chinese Medicine and Feng Shui, this book presents practical techniques and insightful wisdom to restore equilibrium within yourself and your surroundings. Explore the interconnectedness of Yin and Yang, and learn how to embrace their transformative energy to enhance vitality, reduce stress, and cultivate lasting inner peace.

With enlightening case studies and step-by-step exercises, this book provides a comprehensive roadmap for harnessing the power of Yin and Yang. Discover how to tap into your innate potential, navigate life's challenges with grace, and experience a renewed sense of purpose and fulfillment.

Whether you're a beginner or a seasoned practitioner, "The Art of Balancing Yin-Yang Energy" offers a holistic approach to well-being, empowering you to create harmony, achieve personal growth, and unlock the true balance within your life. Dive into this extraordinary guide and embark on a journey toward a harmonious existence today!

Balancing yin-yang energy can bring about numerous benefits in various aspects of life. Here are the top 20 benefits:

1. Harmony and Balance: Balancing yin-yang energy promotes a sense of harmony and balance within oneself and in relationships with others.

2. Enhanced Well-being: Balanced yin-yang energy contributes to overall physical, mental, and emotional well-being.

3. Stress Reduction: Maintaining balanced yin-yang energy helps reduce stress and promotes a state of calmness and relaxation.

4. Increased Energy: Balancing yin-yang energy enhances vitality and boosts energy levels.

5. Emotional Stability: Harmonizing yin-yang energy supports emotional stability, reducing mood swings and promoting emotional resilience.

6. Improved Focus and Clarity: Balanced yin-yang energy enhances mental clarity, concentration, and focus.

7. Better Decision-Making: When yin-yang energy is in equilibrium, it fosters better decision-making skills and promotes sound judgment.

8. Enhanced Intuition: Balancing yin-yang energy can amplify intuition and inner wisdom.

9. Improved Relationships: Harmonizing yin-yang energy cultivates healthier and more balanced relationships, promoting understanding and cooperation.

10. Greater Creativity: Balanced yin-yang energy can enhance creativity and innovation in various aspects of life.

11. Physical Healing: Balancing yin-yang energy supports the body's natural healing abilities and can contribute to faster recovery from illnesses or injuries.

12. Emotional Healing: Harmonizing yin-yang energy aids in emotional healing and facilitates the release of emotional blockages.

13. Enhanced Digestion: Balanced yin-yang energy promotes optimal digestion and helps alleviate digestive issues.

14. Hormonal Balance: Balancing yin-yang energy can help regulate hormonal imbalances and improve overall hormonal health.

15. Improved Sleep Quality: Harmonized yin-yang energy promotes better sleep quality and can help alleviate sleep disorders.

16. Increased Adaptability: Balanced yin-yang energy enhances adaptability and resilience in the face of life's challenges and changes.

17. Strengthened Immune System: Harmonizing yin-yang energy supports a strong immune system, helping the body fend off illnesses and infections.

18. Emotional Resilience: Balanced yin-yang energy fosters emotional resilience, enabling individuals to navigate challenging situations with grace and composure.

19. Enhanced Self-Awareness: Balancing yin-yang energy deepens self-awareness and promotes a greater understanding of oneself.

20. Spiritual Growth: Harmonizing yin-yang energy can facilitate spiritual growth and connection, leading to a sense of purpose and fulfillment.

It's important to note that the benefits of balancing yin-yang energy can be subjective and may vary from individual to individual.

· · · · • · • · · ·

5 KEY TAKEAWAYS FROM EACH CHAPTER

1. Key Takeaways from the chapter on Introduction to Yin-Yang:

1. Understanding Yin-Yang Energy: Yin-Yang energy represents the balance of life itself. It encompasses the dualities found in nature and within ourselves, such as day and night, light and darkness, and male and female energies.

2. Yin Energy: Yin energy is associated with feminine qualities like beauty, compassion, patience, nurturing, and family orientation. When Yin energy is imbalanced or suppressed, it can hinder the manifestation of goals and desires, even if positive affirmations are used.

3. Yang Energy: Yang energy represents masculine qualities such as decisiveness, goal orientation, focus, career drive, and physical strength. If Yang energy is suppressed or imbalanced, it can obstruct career success and limit the ability to take advantage of opportunities.

4. Imbalance and Suppression: Imbalances in Yin and Yang energies can occur, leading to struggles in personal and professional aspects of life. For example, an overactivated Yin energy and suppressed Yang energy may result in being easily suppressed or taken advantage of, while an overactivated Yang energy and suppressed Yin energy can lead to insensitivity and dominance.

5. Activating Both Energies: Activating and balancing both Yin and Yang energies is crucial for overall success and well-being. By recognizing and working on these energies, individuals can achieve a harmonious and

fulfilling life, where personal and professional realms thrive simultaneously.

By implementing the principles of balancing Yin-Yang energy, readers can unlock their full potential, achieve success, and become the best version of themselves.

2. Key Takeaways from the chapter on Impact Of Yin-Yang Frequency:

1. Understanding Yin-Yang Energy: Yin-Yang energy represents the balance between feminine (Yin) and masculine (Yang) qualities. Emotions and energies can also be categorized into Yin and Yang, similar to positive and negative emotions.

2. Imbalance and Its Impact: Imbalance in Yin and Yang energies can lead to struggles in various aspects of life. When Yin energy is suppressed or Yang energy is overly activated, it can affect relationships, personal fulfillment, and the ability to take action towards goals.

3. Identifying Energy Imbalances: By observing a person's behavior, attire, and relationships, one can make an initial assessment of their energy balance. Yin energy is associated

with qualities like beauty, sensitivity, compassion, and caring, while Yang energy is linked to practicality, decision-making, ambition, and assertiveness.

4. Effects of Imbalanced Energy in Relationships: Imbalanced energies can impact relationships. For example, a woman with high Yang energy may struggle to attract romantic partners due to her boyish demeanor and insensitivity. Similarly, a man with high Yin energy may face challenges in taking action and may feel emotional and easily taken for granted.

5. Importance of Balancing Yin and Yang: Activating and balancing both Yin and Yang energies is essential for overall success and fulfillment. Suppressing or neglecting either energy can hinder personal and professional growth. Balancing Yin-Yang energy allows individuals to harmonize their personal and professional lives, leading to greater satisfaction and achievement.

Understanding the dynamics of Yin-Yang energy and striving for a harmonious balance can lead to transformative changes, enabling individuals to live a more fulfilling and purpose-driven life.

3. Key Takeaways from the chapter on 3-Steps To Balance Your Energy:

1. Recognize Missing Qualities: Identify the Yin and Yang qualities that are absent within you and may be contributing to your struggles. Categorize these qualities and acknowledge their importance in attracting goals and achieving success.

2. Make Affirmations: Create affirmations based on the missing qualities you have identified. For example, if you lack sensitivity or spend less time on personal grooming, affirmations like "I love being sensitive towards others" or "I enjoy taking time to look my best every day" can help activate and embrace those qualities.

3. Practice Affirmations with Body Language: Stand in front of a mirror and repeat your affirmations ten times while using body language that aligns with the statements. Connect with the feelings and energy associated with the affirmations to feel empowered and confident.

4. Display Affirmations and Listen to Recordings: Write down your affirmations and display them in visible

places around your house. Additionally, record your affirmations in your own voice and listen to them regularly, embedding them into your subconscious mind. Listen to the recordings during daily activities like showering, cooking, or driving.

5. Take Small Actions Every Day: Take small actions to activate the energy you desire. For instance, if you want to enhance Yin energy, engage in activities like buying makeup or skincare products to embrace your femininity. If you aim to boost Yang energy, take assertive actions, make decisions, or work out to cultivate your masculine traits. Start with small steps and gradually progress to bigger changes.

By recognizing missing qualities, making affirmations, practicing with body language, and taking consistent actions, you can activate and balance your Yin and Yang energies, leading to personal growth, improved relationships, and greater success in various areas of life.

4. Key Takeaways from the chapter on Balance In Different Situations:

1. Recognizing the Importance of Balancing Yin and Yang: Understand the significance of using Yin energy (sensitivity, forgiveness, emotions) and Yang energy (being disciplined, practical, assertive) in different situations. Recognize that both energies have their place and knowing when to use each is crucial.

2. Four Styles for Balancing Energies: The chapter introduces four styles: Turtle, Shark, Teddy Bear, and Owl. Each style represents a different combination of Yin and Yang energies and has unique qualities and emotions associated with it.

3. Choosing the Right Style: Determine which style to adopt by asking yourself, "What is more important, goal or relationship?" Based on the situation, choose the appropriate style that aligns with your priorities at that moment.

4. Understanding the Styles:

- Turtle: A passive style with low emphasis on both relationships and goals. Passive, fearful, and seeks security. Use when conflicts arise or to maintain inner security.

- Shark: An aggressive style focused on goals, lacking Yin energy. Assertive, ambitious, and seeks control. Use when achieving goals is more important than relationships.

- Teddy Bear: A nurturing style emphasizing relationships, lacking Yang energy. Submissive, caring, and sacrifices for others. Use when relationships are prioritized over goals.

- Owl: An assertive style that balances Yin and Yang energies. Calm, conflict-friendly, and seeks win-win outcomes. Use when both goals and relationships are equally important.

5. Practicing and Adapting Styles: Regularly practice and refine your ability to choose the appropriate style based on the situation. Learn to shuffle between styles quickly and adapt to different frequencies. Emphasize frequency over understanding and continue practicing to achieve mastery.

5. Key Takeaways from the chapter on Balancing Yin-Yang Energy & Practical Application:

1. Recap of Lessons: Recap the key lessons learned, such as preparing for a Law of Attraction lifestyle, focusing on upgrading frequency rather than understanding, surrendering to the universe, emotional habit tracking, Advanced Attraction lifestyle, FDBA integration, powerful words, values, priorities, and the purpose of life.

2. Importance of Values: Understand the significance of values and how they influence our behavior. Differentiate between real values (leading to good qualities) and artificial values (leading to negative qualities). Upgrade values by dropping borrowed values, affirming new values, and dedicating resources to support them.

3. Emotions and Priorities: Recognize that the purpose of life is to experience emotions, both positive and negative. Learn to prioritize emotions and create easy conditions for positive emotions while making it difficult to feel negative emotions.

4. Yin-Yang Energy: Recap the importance of balancing Yin and Yang energies. Review the concept of recognizing missing qualities, making affirmations for those qualities, and taking small actions every day. Understand the practical application of different styles (turtle, shark, teddy bear, and owl) to match Yin-Yang energy in various life situations.

5. Emphasize Recap for Retention: Stress the importance of recap to prevent forgetting valuable lessons. Regularly revisit and reinforce the knowledge gained to ensure effective integration and application in daily life.

6. Key Takeaways from the chapter on Understanding 7-Energy Chakras:

1. Balancing Yin Yang Energies: Understanding the correlation between Yin Yang energy and the activation of the seven chakras is crucial for achieving balance. By activating these chakras, both Yin and Yang energies can be fully harnessed.

2. Root Chakra: The foundation of emotions lies in the root chakra. If this chakra is deactivated, it can lead to insecurity, low confidence, and a lack of motivation to work

towards goals. Activating the root chakra is essential for building self-confidence and taking action.

3. Sacral Chakra: The sacral chakra is associated with desire and emotions. When this chakra is low, individuals may struggle to feel strongly positive or negative emotions. Activation of the sacral chakra is necessary for experiencing passion, ambition, and emotional control.

4. Solar Plexus Chakra: The solar plexus chakra influences self-esteem and the immune system. Low activation of this chakra can lead to a lack of self-respect and difficulty in respecting others. Activating the solar plexus chakra allows for greater self-confidence and healthy relationships with others.

5. Heart Chakra: The heart chakra serves as a bridge between Yin and Yang energies. Activating this chakra opens up both sides and facilitates the experience and expression of love. When the heart chakra is deactivated, individuals may struggle to receive or give love, hindering personal growth and fulfillment.

Note: These key takeaways provide a brief summary of the chapter's content. For a comprehensive understanding and practical implementation, it is recommended to refer to the complete chapter.

7. Key Takeaways from the chapter on Sound Meditation For Chakra Activation:

1. Chakra Activation: Learn the sound and affirmation associated with each chakra to effectively activate and energize them. By humming the specific sound for each chakra, you can stimulate and align the energy centers within your body.

2. Root Chakra Activation: Use the sound "LUM" to activate the root chakra, which is responsible for confidence, stability, and taking responsibility for your emotions. Focus on feeling the vibration at the base of your spine.

3. Sacral Chakra Activation: Humming "VAM" activates the sacral chakra, associated with emotions, passion, and pleasure. This chakra activation enhances your ability to experience and manage your emotions effectively.

4. Solar Plexus Chakra Activation: The sound "RAM" activates the solar plexus chakra, responsible for self-esteem

and personal power. By humming this sound, you can boost your self-respect and cultivate confidence.

5. Heart Chakra Activation: Use the sound "YAM" to activate the heart chakra, which governs love, compassion, and connection. By humming this sound, you can enhance your ability to give and receive love, creating harmonious relationships.

Note: These key takeaways provide a brief summary of the chapter's content. For a comprehensive understanding and practical implementation, it is recommended to refer to the complete chapter.

8. Key Takeaways from the chapter on Energy Charging Exercise For 7-Chakras:

1. Energy Chakra Charging Exercise: This exercise teaches how to energize and activate the chakras for maximum benefit and transformation in life. It is an ancient practice found in Chinese medicine and Indian mythology, known to cure ailments and promote overall health.

2. Chakras and Energy: Our body is made of energy, and when the energy in our chakras diminishes, illness can

manifest. Activating and charging the chakras can heal the body and boost the immune system.

3. Physical Movements: The exercise involves specific hand movements in coordination with breath and visualization. These movements generate and direct energy through the chakras, creating a wave-like flow from the solar plexus to the crown chakra and back down to the root chakra.

4. Affirmations and Energy Balls: Along with the movements, affirmations are spoken to align intentions with the chakras. Energy balls are created and charged with the affirmation "I am God, We are all God," symbolizing the connection to the divine.

5. Daily Practice: Consistency is key. Practicing this exercise daily for five minutes can activate and recharge the chakras, leading to profound changes in one's life. Increased energy, inner peace, and a sense of gratitude are among the transformative effects reported.

Note: These key takeaways provide a brief summary of the chapter's content. For a comprehensive understanding and practical implementation, it is recommended to refer to the complete chapter.

9. Key Takeaways from the chapter on Shiva: The Masculine & Feminine Energy Together:

1. Brighu's Devotion: Brighu, one of Shiva's disciples, became intensely devoted to Shiva, embodying feminine qualities. This devotion led to a tiff between Parvati, Shiva's wife, and Brighu.

2. Shiva as the Adi Yogi: Shiva is seen as the first yogi and guru in yoga philosophy. The practice of yoga and its availability today is attributed to Parvati's influence on Shiva, compelling him to teach others.

3. Brighu's Devotional Actions: Brighu insisted on circumambulating Shiva three times every day, ignoring Parvati. This devotion expressed intense dedication but lacked logical reasoning.

4. Parvati's Response: Parvati challenged Brighu's discrimination and refusal to acknowledge her presence. In response, Brighu transformed into a mouse and later a bird to go around Shiva alone.

5. Shiva's Lesson: Shiva, amused by Brighu's devotion and Parvati's involvement, merged Parvati into himself

and assumed a dual-gender form. Shiva wanted Brighu to recognize the wholeness of existence, and Brighu eventually circumambulated both aspects of Shiva's being.

Note: These key takeaways provide a brief summary of the chapter's content. For a comprehensive understanding, it is recommended to refer to the complete chapter.

10. Key Takeaways from the chapter on Yin-Yang And Taoism:

1. Yin Yang Balance: Taoism emphasizes the importance of balance and living in alignment with the Tao. Yin yang represents the coexistence and interplay of contrasting forces and elements in the universe, such as dark and light, weak and strong, soft and hard.

2. Harmony and Harmony: Unlike the Western concept of dualism, yin and yang are not in conflict but complement and work harmoniously together. They fit seamlessly, representing the harmonious interplay of opposites.

3. Five Phases and Transformation: The yin yang principle is associated with the Chinese philosophy of the five phases or elements (wood, fire, metal, water, earth) and

their continuous interchange. These phases describe the transformations in nature and the cyclical nature of existence.

4. Masculine and Feminine Energies: Yin yang is often symbolized as the masculine and feminine energies in life, but it is important to note that these energies are not strictly defined by gender. Yin represents receptivity and softness, while yang represents action and strength. Both energies exist in all individuals and life forms.

5. Optimism and Resilience: Understanding the yin yang principle can bring optimism and resilience to life. It teaches that everything has its opposite and is understood by contrast. By embracing the ebb and flow of life and accepting the harmony of yin yang, one can navigate challenges with grace and appreciate the balance within the universe.

Note: These key takeaways provide a condensed summary of the chapter. For a comprehensive understanding, it is recommended to refer to the complete chapter.

Chapter One
INTRODUCTION TO YIN-YANG

"Yin and yang are not opposing forces; they are complementary. They need each other to exist."
- Karen Madwell

In this book, we are going to talk about a very powerful technique called balancing Yin Yang energy. Most people have no idea what this energy is, and that is why I wanted to introduce this with the help of this book. If you want to learn what this crazy energy called Yin Yang energy balance is, how it helps us achieve our goals, and why sometimes we are not able to achieve our goals when our

Yin energy is imbalanced. How do we really attract our goals using your Yin Yang energy balance? Let's understand that concept first. What is Yin Yang energy? You must have seen this amazing Chinese symbol that kind of looks like a circle like this.

This energy symbol is nothing but the balance of life itself, which means there is a day, there is a night, there is light, there is darkness, there is a male, there is a female. So in Yin Yang energy, it is discovered through scientific research that all of us are made of energy. And because we are made of energy, there are two kinds of energies within us. One is called Yin energy, and the second is called Yang energy. Yin energy is like female energy, and

Yang energy is like male energy. For example, Yin energy is made of qualities related to women, I'm not saying men don't have these qualities, I'm just saying women have these qualities more. For example, "beauty". It's a word more related to female energy rather than male energy. "Caring", and "emotional behavior", are right between men and women. I'm not saying men are not emotional but women are more emotional and also more family oriented. You'll observe who sacrifices more for family women or men. No, it's not the men; it's the women who sacrifice more for the family. Women have "patience", women are "compassionate", women are "protective", "nurturing" etc. Kind all of these words are related to the word female energy, now let's understand something amazing. If there's a girl who is doing affirmations that "I'm very very happy in my married life" but her Yin energy is suppressed, do you think her affirmations for marriage will work? No. Because the yin energy is suppressed but let's say by chance she gets married right and now she's saying I'm happily married which means she's married but she now wants to be happily married but she's missing qualities like compassion, she's missing qualities like caring, family orientation, love, kindness, emotional. If she is married will she have a happy married life? No. So some people ask me Sooraj, why my affirmations are not working for me and I always ask them to check their yin-yang frequency balance. Is your yin and yang energy both activated? And I'll give you an example of how to check if they are not. I will be teaching in a very practical way of understanding whether your yin energy is activated or not. Whether your yang energy is activated or not.

Can you guess the examples of Yang's energy qualities? Yang are male qualities which I'm not saying women don't have but some qualities which are more related to male more. For example "decision makers" males are the head of the family, they're supposed to be aggressive, "goal-oriented", "focused", and "career-oriented". "Anger" is a common emotion between males and females. Women are strong but strength is not their main quality. Strength is a main quality for men, which is physical strength. Men are "insensitive" and "hard-working".

Now think there's a man or a boy who's doing affirmations "I'm making one lakh rupees a month" or " I'm making five lakh rupees a month" or "I have a million dollar business", whatever affirmations they're making about their career but if they are Yang energy qualities are suppressed they cannot achieve anything. I believe that Yang or Yin energy can never be killed, nobody can kill your energies, and it is just suppressed. So if a boy's Yang energy is suppressed his affirmations are not going to work. Will this person attract career goals? No. Or even if they do attract career goals, they will not be able to take complete advantage of those career goals.

As we discussed, Yin energy was personal life-oriented, similarly Yang energy is Professional life oriented. If a person is struggling in both areas of their life it means their both energies are suppressed.

Someone can have one type of energy more and another type of energy in a negligible amount. It is called the imbalance of energies. I'll give you one more example, let's say there's a girl whose Yin energy is over-activated and Yang energy is suppressed, she will be easily suppressed by other people, other people will take advantage of her, and people will be able to abuse her.

Now let's look at the other example. There is a boy who has over-activated Yang energy but under-activated Yin energy. Now what will happen to this boy? He will be too insensitive, he will start getting physically abusive towards people, he will be emotionally and verbally abusive towards people, he will not give people a chance to take decisions, and he will try to dominate all the time himself.

In my case, when I started this journey for the first time I was more suffering in my Yang energy because this was suppressed for me, so I was suffering a lot in my professional life. My affirmations were not working; my law of attraction was not working, in fact, after some time both got suppressed. So I started even failing in my personal life, it was only when my mentor made me realize the way to activate both these energies, I worked on these energies and I really started becoming successful in my life. So if you check me in my life today my personal life is also successful and my professional life is also successful. I feel balanced in my life, my Yin energy is also activated and my Yang energy is also activated.

This is a scientific concept proven in science, proven in physics. We need to start activating both our energies to be successful and to be the best version of ourselves.

· · · ● · · ● · · ·

Chapter Two
IMPACT OF YIN-YANG FREQUENCY

"In the midst of chaos, there is also opportunity."
- Sun Tzu

In this chapter, we are going to learn about something so powerful that will transform your life. Not for a couple of days but for the rest of your life. Because once you activate this lesson, your life just completely goes to the next level. What is this lesson? It is about the Yin Yang frequency balance. Universe has given us two types of energies, the same as we have two types of emotions. What are the two types of emotions? Positive emotions and negative emotions. But emotions are basically just feelings, right? Similarly, energy is also of two types Yin Energy and Yang Energy. Now, I'll give you a quick story about this to understand this very fast, in a very easy and very practical way. There was one lady who came to me once for coaching. A very senior lady from a corporate company. When she entered my office for the first time, I saw that she was about 5ft eight inches. She was about three inches taller than me, very strong body and she was wearing jeans, a t-shirt, and boy cut hairstyle, her voice was very very strong. So whenever I meet people, I start predicting which energy they have more. Do they have Yin energy more? Or do they have the Yang energy? So for example, Yin energy is the female energy, and Yang energy is known as the male energy. What are the qualities of female and male energy? I'll tell you some quick qualities that will make it easy for you to understand. Female qualities are qualities that don't mean that men don't have, but it is more relevant to ladies. So for example here, beauty is related to females. But do you think the word beauty is related to men? Not really, handsome, maybe, but definitely not beautiful, females are more sensitive while males are more practical. How? Women are more emotional whereas men are a little insensitive; men are a little more practical. Can you understand that? If you take example if you take two children, one girl, and one boy, and you give both of them a doll, and you come after half an hour, what will you find? What will the girl are doing with the doll? She would be making her hair, she's doing makeup, and she's making the doll more beautiful. What the boy would be doing with the doll? You will find the doll completely broken in the boy's hand. Boys are a little crazy because they're a little insensitive.

Females are caring while males are careless. For example, you're walking on the road and there's a lady and a man walking on the road, and there's a dog who's got hurt. How will the girls react? Girls will try to help the dog while the boys will be like- let's move on. But it doesn't mean that all men are like that. I'm just saying that this is more girls' oriented feelings and more boys' oriented qualities. Similarly, men are more work-oriented. Is that right or wrong? It's right. Because that's how the universe has made us with Yin and Yang energy. For Example, many years ago when we started humanity. If you observe, human beings were not human beings. Once upon a time, we were animals. How many of you remember this? Have you learned in school? We were monkeys. We were animals. And then from monkeys, we converted into human beings over a period of time. The transformation happened when we became human beings. The woman would sit in the cave, taking care of the cave, which is the house, and the man's responsibility was to go out hunting. So getting food was a man's responsibility. If you tell the woman to go and hunt, will she do the hunting? She'll say "I can't do killing at all". These women are more sensitive and more emotional. You bring the food home, and she'll cook for you, but she does not go and kill. Is that clear? For generations, we have been like this; the universe has given us some powerful qualities. In qualities to women, Yang qualities to men.

But within us, we have which energy? Only Yin or Yang, or both? We will always have both. But what will be your strong energy? Depending on if you're a woman or a man.

Coming back to this beautiful story, this lady came inside my house in this office. I looked at her attire; she has a very strong personality. Which energy do you think she was practicing more? She was practicing Yin energy more, or was she practicing male energy more quickly? But I can't assume that. So I started asking her some questions. When she sat here in front of me. I said, Ma'am, is it okay before you tell me about what problem you've come for, can I ask you some questions? She said yes. I said, just tell me if I'm right or wrong, okay? I'm not sure. I'm just asking questions. Ma'am, is it true that when you were a very young child in your house, at a very early age, you had to take on a lot of responsibilities? Is it true? She said yes. How do you know? I said I'm not sure. I'm just checking with you. She said yes. Why did I ask this question? Because when at an early age, she had to take on more responsibilities, which energy she had to activate? The Yang energy! The practical part, the work orientation, the decision making, the aggressiveness, she had to activate that. And then I asked her, in school, did you have more friends who were girls, or did you have more friends who were boys? If I'm not wrong, do you have more friends who are boys? Yes! She said, but how do you know? I'll tell you how. Attraction happens between Yin energy and Yang energy. Not between Yin and Yin or Yang and Yang. So, in school, the reason she attracted boys more, was because even though she's a girl, within her, she was activating

Yang's energy. So boys would get close to her, and she would get close to boys, and they would find each other very comfortable because Yang and Yang's energy can become friends, but there cannot be an attraction between them. Correct? Girls did not get attracted to her. Girls found her Boyish, Masculine, Insensitive, Too harsh, and Very aggressive. That is why other girls wouldn't get close to this girl. Then later I asked her, when you got into college, did it ever happen with you that you got close to a guy and you felt dramatically involved with him, but later the boy told you that he's just good friends with you, he doesn't feel like that about you? She said yes. How do you know that? It's very simple. Because boys would get very close to you because you are their buddy. But will they get romantic with this girl? No, because the yang energy was up there, they couldn't feel that beauty because the same energy can't attract. She was a very senior lady, she was in her 50s. So I asked her, if I'm not wrong, you're married now. She said yes, I am. And I said, if I'm not wrong, you're very successful in your career. She said, yes. She was successful because her Yang energy was very good. And I asked her, if I'm not wrong, people are scared of you, right? Especially men are scared of you. She said, yeah, I don't take bullshit from

THE ART OF BALANCING YIN-YANG ENERGY

people. Now, does she need this energy to be successful in the corporate world? Yes or no? Yeah, she needed it. That's why she practiced it. But then I asked her, I said, if I'm not wrong, the marriage that you had, had you had a love marriage or an arranged marriage? In her case? She said it's an arranged marriage. I said, but if I'm not wrong, you're very successful in your corporate life, but you're struggling in your married life. She just didn't fall out of a chair. She said, how do you know all this about me? I said I'm not sure. I'm just asking questions. Just tell me yes or no. She said, yes, she was struggling with her husband. And I said, if I'm not wrong, you find your husband very weak. She again said yes. He's not strong enough. He doesn't stand up for himself. He doesn't take responsibility in his life. I said, if I'm not wrong, your husband is not successful in his career . He's using Affirmations maybe for his career, but he's not getting results. She said, how do you know?

Can you guess why the husband is not successful? And why is he weak? Which energy has the husband activated? His Yin energy is activated and his Yang energy is suppressed. Why is she struggling with him? Because her Yin energy is suppressed. Her Yang energy is high. In both of them, their Yin and Yang energy was unbalanced. I asked her another question. Do you have children? She said yes. I have a son. He's grown up. I said, if I'm not wrong, your son has broken up with his girlfriend or he's divorced or he's struggling in his relationships with girls. She said, how do you know he's divorced? Let me tell you the answer, the boy grows up in a family of imbalanced parents where the woman is Yang, the man is Yin. The mother is Yang, the father is Yin. He's brought up his entire life in imbalanced energy. The woman of the house is actually the man of the house. So will she allow this boy to become Yang's energy unconsciously? Not consciously, a. She will be the man of the house. Do you know some families like this? And they never allow the men to make decisions.

So what happens is the boy's Yang energy gets suppressed. So when he grows up and gets close to girls, girls will become friends with him. But will they be attracted to him? No. So that means he will struggle in his personal life. That is how I predicted that he was struggling. Believe it or not. She said her husband or her son's wife; she said nothing is wrong with us. We are very good friends. I just don't feel like I love you. We just don't feel that attraction. And they got divorced. And here is what I'm trying to convey. An imbalanced couple produces an Imbalanced son. This imbalanced son tomorrow will get married to what kind of a person? The balanced person or the imbalanced person? An Imbalanced person. Because he is also imbalanced, he will attract imbalanced people when he gets married. What kind of children will he produce? Hands again. Balance or imbalance? Imbalance. It means your Imbalance will attract negative frequency and imbalance frequency not only for you but for your future generations. I'm not joking about this. This sounds scary, but this is true. Your future generations get impacted because of the frequency that you are imbalanced with. The story that I told you. You can relate to that story here right now?

Woman with high Yang energy:

If you are a woman realizing that your yang energy is too high or your Yin energy is suppressed, in your personal life you may be struggling. You may be struggling in your relationships. If you're married, you have a problem going on with the physical intimacy part of your relationship. You may be successful in your career, which means you are very good at what you do. And you're proud of it. And you know that people cannot take you for granted. You're a very strong personality, you don't like gossip conversations.

But most women like gossip, right? You don't like gossip because you're not a woman. You are a woman with Yang energy mode, when you go shopping, you buy and come back, and you don't waste any time. Most women do window shopping for two to 3 hours. You find it a waste of time. You never go out with those women. You may have lost touch with your girlfriends who talk unnecessary gossip. You have lost touch with your school friends, your college friends who talk unnecessary gossip. You cannot relate to them anymore. You find getting ready to make up and all a waste of time, it's nonsense. And you tell people many times, to accept me the way I am. You become more like a boy. You're insensitive like a boy. You're a decision-maker like a boy. You don't like doing makeup like a boy, you do shopping like a boy, you talk like a boy, and you're aggressive like a boy. And then you feel hurt that people are not attracted. You don't like crying in front of people. But you do cry alone. You feel hurt, and you never tell people about what you feel. And you're a very short-tempered person.

So what do you need to do? What is the solution? You may be thinking that surpassing Yang can be a solution. No, don't suppress the Yang. You worked very hard to activate your Yang energy. You become strong because of it. You because your life is successful because of the Yang energy today. So don't suppress it. So what do we do? So the Yang is already high. What do we do now? We will activate the yin.

Boy with high Yin energy:

If you are a boy with less Yang and more Yin energy. You're more emotional than necessary, you have very big goals, but you're not able to take action. You're lazy. You get frustrated. Why are you not able to take action? So sometimes what you do is you just drop your goals. You think I'll become spiritual, but actually, you're running away from your goals. The fact is you want to achieve your goals, but you're not able to take action in life. Second prediction about you. You are very emotional. People can easily take you for granted, and then you feel bad. You do a lot for people, but people don't do enough for you. And then you feel heard about it. And that happens in your family also. You are the one who's doing everything for everybody. But you are the one who everybody forgets. They forget your birthday. They don't find a very beautiful gift for you. They don't give surprises to you. They give a surprise to somebody else in the family who's hardly doing anything. Why? Because your Yang energy is suppressed. You're not aggressive. You don't know how to say no. You end up saying yes to everything. And then you feel bad and then people take you for granted. And then you always end up doing more and paid less. Your clients take you for granted. Your office takes you for granted. Your boss takes you for granted. People call you emotional fools. You're doing affirmations for succeeding in your professional life. Will their affirmations work for them? It will not work for them. Why? Because there is an Imbalance going on. The required energy is missing. What do I mean by the required energy is missing? Aggressiveness, decision-making, hard-working, practical work, orientation, saying nowhere you have to say no. All those qualities are missing. So the action frequency is missing. Four levels of frequency we talk about in advanced contraction. Everyone thinks I say feelings, thoughts, beliefs, and actions. If these energies are missing, which frequency will get blocked? Feelings, thoughts, beliefs, etc. When your energy is at an oppressed action frequency, you will not be able to take the required action.

High Yin and Yang energy:

If the Yin energy is too high, will these ladies attract men who are healthy men or unhealthy men? Will they attract men who are respectful or disrespectful towards women? Will they attract men who are always taking care of women or getting abusive towards women? Because the Yin energy is too much, they will attract men who are very Yang overactive. So men, who are overly ambitious, which means very high Yang energy, will be very insensitive, very disrespectful towards women. They will use bad words. They will even physically move their hands on women. Why? Because of Too much energy. This is also a different kind of imbalance. If your Yin-Yang energy is imbalanced, you might achieve your goals, but you will find life is Meaningless because your purpose in life will never be fulfilled if you use your energy. Similarly, this can be with men also.

Yang energy is responsible for your professional life and Yin is responsible for your personal life. Many people are a little confused here. Sometimes they think their Yin is suppressed and sometimes they think Yang is suppressed. There's a **third category of people** who are confused.

That means your yin is also suppressed a little bit and your yang is also suppressed and the proof is both your areas are struggling.

Yin-Yang Quality Chart:

Yin	Yang	Yin	Yang
Feminine	Masculine	Yin organs (e.g., kidneys, liver)	Yang organs (e.g., heart, lungs)
Dark	Light	Yin organs (e.g., spleen, stomach)	Yang organs (e.g., small intestine, large intestine)
Passive	Active	Yin meridians (e.g., kidney meridian)	Yang meridians (e.g., bladder meridian)
Cold	Hot	Yin colors (e.g., black, purple)	Yang colors (e.g., white, red)
Slow	Fast	Yin energy (inward, contracting)	Yang energy (outward, expanding)
Intuitive	Logical	Yin direction (downward)	Yang direction (upward)
Receptive	Assertive	Yin emotions (e.g., sadness, fear)	Yang emotions (e.g., joy, anger)
Restful	Energetic	Yin elements (e.g., water, earth)	Yang elements (e.g., fire, metal)
Subtle	Bold	Yin weather (e.g., rain, fog)	Yang weather (e.g., sunshine, wind)
Soft	Hard	Yin time (night)	Yang time (day)
Quiet	Loud	Yin taste (e.g., salty, sour)	Yang taste (e.g., sweet, spicy)
Nurturing	Protective	Yin body parts (e.g., lower body, joints)	Yang body parts (e.g., upper body, muscles)
Moon	Sun	Yin season (winter)	Yang season (summer)
Water	Fire	Yin qualities in nature (e.g., stillness, hibernation)	Yang qualities in nature (e.g., growth, blossoming)
Yin symbol (broken line in the I Ching hexagram)	Yang symbol (solid line in the I Ching hexagram)	Yin spirituality (introspection, meditation)	Yang spirituality (active rituals, ceremonies)

Note: these qualities are not fixed and can be understood and interpreted differently in various contexts and philosophies.

· · · ● · ● · · ·

Chapter Three
3-STEPS TO BALANCE YOUR ENERGY

"Everything contains its opposite. Yin and yang are complementary forces, interdependent and interconnected in the natural world."
- Dan Millman

Now, let's get to leaning toward how you can really activate your Yin and Yang energy! Both.

Step 1: Recognize Missing Qualities

Step number one is a very critical step, which is to **recognize missing qualities.** Now, what qualities am I talking about? Qualities that are required to practice either the Yin energy or the Yang energy. The reason one is struggling in his/her life may be the Yang energy, maybe he/she is not aggressive enough to take action towards their goals. They are not hardworking enough to take action toward their goals, or the reason for their struggle may be their Yin qualities, which means being more emotional, and sensitive towards people, is missing in them. So they get angry very fast. They hurt people too fast, and then they say, "I was telling the truth, what I can do?" They are a little insensitive. They aren't very sensitive. Now look inside you for these missing qualities. Are you realizing that's why you're struggling in your personal life?

Take a blank page and Write down those Yin and Yang qualities which are absent inside you. Write down the male and female qualities you are missing in you. I want you to recognize and write some of the Yin and Yang qualities which are missing in you, suppressed in you, which you require to attract goals in your life. You may have gotten feedback many times from your family and friends for the qualities which you need to have. Those are the qualities I'm talking about. You just have to categorize them either as Yin energy or Yang energy. Nothing else.

Even if you do 20% of this exercise correctly, your life will start changing. I promise you that. You don't need more clarity from me. You just need to practice this in your head. Put some stress on your brain and say- what Yin qualities are missing in me? What Yang qualities are missing in me?

Step 2: Make Affirmations

Now make affirmations for those missing qualities. This is a very critical step. For example, suppose a lady realizes that one of the Yin qualities is missing in her, she doesn't like wasting time in getting ready. She does get ready for occasions, but on a daily basis, she doesn't like to waste time getting ready. So her new affirmation should be "I love getting ready". "I love doing makeup every day". Now, does it mean she has to look like Katrina Kaif every day? No, she doesn't. But is it good to look good every day? Is there something wrong with that? No, nothing's wrong with that. Beauty is a word related to women. God has given her that superpower. Why wouldn't she want to do it? I'll tell you why. When her Yin energy is suppressed, women don't feel beautiful on the inside. And when she doesn't feel beautiful on the inside, she doesn't feel like looking more beautiful on the outside. When you don't feel that beauty inside, you don't feel like putting in the effort of looking beautiful on the outside. So if she keeps telling people to accept her the way she is, that's not going to work. Why? If she wants people to accept her first, she has to accept her beauty first. She has to take care of her beauty first. Then people get attracted to her, not otherwise. So if you are a lady and do so, make that affirmation right now- "I love getting ready".

Similarly, suppose a man realizes he is not comfortable saying no. He is not comfortable asking for money. So what happens is, he gives money to people, and they don't return money back to him. He should write down affirmations, like: "I love saying no to people comfortably".

You've understood how to make Affirmations Based on basic lost action goals or regarding any of your missing qualities. Grab your pen and make some affirmations for your Yin and Yang qualities

Here's one more exercise. Stand up in front of a mirror and repeat this affirmation ten times. Whichever affirmations you've made right now, repeat it ten times. But when you say the affirmation, you have to use your body language which connects with that affirmation. Connect your body language to that statement, feel those feelings, feel the energy inside you, and keep repeating. You will start feeling strong and energetic.

You can never kill the energy. It's always there. All you need to do is activate it and these are the steps activating it. For example, if there is diesel that you have not used for ten years, what do you need to use that diesel? A spark or a huge fire? A Spark! The yin energy within women and the Yang energy within men are like unlimited potential inside. You just need to ignite it with a spark. If you spark it a little bit in the next few days, you'll see amazing things happening to you. I promise you that people will start giving you confidence that you've become different. So keep practicing these affirmations every day. Display these affirmations in as many places in your house as you can. Record them in your own voice. Listen to them as many times as you can when you're in the shower, when you're cooking, when you're driving, riding a bike, or driving a car. Listen to these affirmations as much as possible. They will become part of your subconscious. If you want, you can even make them part of your daily practice.

Step 3: Take Small Action Everyday

Now, we are coming to the next step which is the most critical step. Now start taking small actions to activate that energy. What small actions? For Example, if you are a girl, which small action can you take before you go to sleep to activate that energy quickly? Many ladies think that at night before sleeping they can go to Amazon and do some shopping. You could do some makeup shopping, Maybe lipstick, maybe eyeliner. Maybe a blush. Buy something that you would have never bought before. Just to activate that Yin energy on a daily basis. Take small actions every day to start activating that Yin energy. Use casual if you need to. Start having fun every day. If you will do your best to accept yourself, to love yourself, to look beautiful tonight, and you will not do it for your husband, you will not do it for your family, you will do it for someone else. You will do it for yourself. Because you love looking beautiful. Because that's how the universe has made you. I'll give you one last example about makeup here. This is especially for ladies who are still going through some resistance about- "I don't want to do this", or "I like myself the way I am". Let me give you an example: If you put a lot of makeup on men, do you really think they start looking good? Yes or no? No. In fact, men look stupid with makeup. Think about a girl, she doesn't have good features, she doesn't look good, and you apply amazing makeup. Then she suddenly starts looking like, wow! Is that possible with girls? Yes or no? Yes! Universe has made you like this. Who are you to reject that?

If you are a boy, what can you do to activate your Yang energy? You may work out. Give yourself that aggressiveness. Take some decisions tonight that you've been pending for a long time. Call up somebody and say no to somebody. Take some decisions; don't take very tough decisions tonight. Take small ones. Remember, take small actions.

A boy who has less Yang energy, if you ask them, what will you eat? What should we order? They will say, you order, or they will say whatever is fine, he should build the courage to say "I will choose". He should also take the menu in his hands and say, "I will order for you today". Is this a small decision or a very life-changing decision? It's a small decision, but don't take life-changing decisions immediately because you need experience with this energy. I hope you have got my point. So please take these actions tonight before you're sleeping tonight. Either it can be working out, or it can be taking a strong decision (Don't take a very big decision, but take a small decision tonight), Calling up and saying no to someone, asking money from someone whom you've given money, Take some action related to that affirmation that you've written tonight before you sleep.

You have to take action to change yourself in the best possible form.

· · · · • · • · · ·

Chapter Four
BALANCE IN DIFFERENT SITUATIONS

"The wise embrace both the light and the dark, understanding the importance of balance and the unity of opposites." - Lao Tzu

In this chapter let's learn a very practical way of balancing your energies so that you understand which energy to use and when. Because in some situations you will need the Yin energy of being sensitive, forgiving, and emotional. And sometimes you need the Yang energy, you need to be hard, you need to be disciplined, sometimes you have to punish people to give them the best results, you have to be practical, and you have to be a little insensitive sometimes.

But you have to understand when to use which Yin and when to use which Yang. This chapter is the formula that will help you to understand, and to choose correctly when to use Yin and when to use Yang energy.

We have created four styles based on the amount of Yin and Yang energies. Each style has a different quality and emotion. Each style contains Yin and Yang energies in different proportions, one style has less Yin while the other one has more, and one style doesn't have Yin while the other one only contains Yin. Let's delve into the chapter and learn about these styles.

We have drawn four squares, each square represents a style. You can also draw this on paper. You should have four boxes like this:

In the bottom right write "High on Goals" and on the top left write "High on Relationships".

Now ask yourself a question: "What is important, goal or relationship?"

Write down this question on the paper and think about the answer for a minute. In any situation of life, what is important? Goal or relationship? Did you get your answer? Sometimes relationships are important and sometimes goals. You can't always have both. So how do you decide? How do you make this decision? Here we use the styles.

In every situation of life, you have to get used to asking yourself this primary question "What is more important? Goal or relationship? According to the moment, the answer will change. Depending on the answer, you have to choose your style of using Yin-Yang energy. There are four styles: turtle, shark, teddy bear, and owl.

1. Turtle:

Style number one is a turtle. The box Turtle style is in the bottom left box. Turtle style is a passive style. If you look at these four boxes on the top left over here it says high on relationships, on the bottom right it says high on goals. By looking at the position of turtle style, what do you think is important in turtle style? Is the relationship important or is the goal important? Check where the relationship word is written, Turtle is very far from it. Check where the goal word is written, Turtle is also very far from it. So it's called low on relationships and also low on goals. And that is why this is called a passive style. What is the passive style? Wherever you go right close to a turtle build a relationship with a turtle. If you meet up for the first time and you're trying to build a relationship with a turtle saying how cute you are, what will the turtle do? It'll go inside its shell. He's like I don't want to talk to you, why are you here? I may be cute, but I don't want to talk to you. So they go inside the shell. So they are low on relationships. If you have a goal to achieve with the turtle what will the turtle do? He'll say, I don't know this business, I am going home. And they will turtle out. So a turtle is somebody who by nature is very passive.

The passive style has an emotional pattern. Generally operating out of fear. Which means they always care for security. They're always looking for security. So they're always feeling insecure in their life. That is their emotional pattern. So the emotional pattern of a passive turtle is always feared. They believe that **conflicts are bad**. They always run away from conflicts. Their need is that they're always looking for certainty in their life. They're always looking for comfort in their life. They're always looking for predictability in their life. They're always looking for assurance in their life. And that is why the result is lost. What is the result of talking to a turtle? Lose. What does "lose" mean? You lose both things, goals, and relationships while dealing with such people because they don't engage with you. For example, you may have had this experience where you have a conflict with one of your friends and you're calling them and they're not picking up your phone only and you got frustrated. Or if they owe you money or anything but they just don't pick up the phone. Why? Their turtle buys time. Is this the right style to apply if you want to attract good things in your life? You may be thinking- "no, it's not a good style to apply. But remember every style is important. You have to ask this question "At this moment, what is more important? Goal or relationship?"

I'll give you an example. Let's say you are a man and you're married. You come home; your wife tells you that she had a fight with your mother. She's also strong and your mother is also very strong. And both of them had a fight. What is the best style to apply right now? Behalf married. Avoid this entire discussion. Mom says anything to you, you shouldn't say anything. Wife says anything to you, what do you do? Listen and don't give any advice. This is where you become a turtle. You become passive. You take care of your inner security. Own account for the clinical. Turtle is a good side.

One more example- In the office, your colleagues are fighting. Why do you want to get into it? You become passive and silent to get out of that unnecessary situation. So, at certain times, you have to neither use too much Yin nor use too much yang. If you observe the turtle, energy is also suppressed and Yang energy is also suppressed.

Now, let's move to the next style,

2. Shark

Look at the high goals box above there is the second style: It's called a shark. The shark style is an aggressive style. What energy is aggressive? The Yang energy. That is only Yang energy; the shark does not contain even a small part of Yin. If you go to a shark, and you say: shark you are so beautiful, can I touch you? Can I play with you? What will the shark do? It can attack you. Sharks don't like relationships. Sharks don't like unnecessary emotions. Sharks don't like getting emotional attacks. Sharks love blood, money, goals, ambition, super ambition. All the time talking about money, all the time talking about work. You can relate to this style, and I am sure that you've become this kind of person. They hardly invest any amount of time in emotions. "Anger is the emotional pattern of the shark". Sharks are mostly very angry, mostly very aggressive, and mostly very angry. Belief patterns of a shark gain control in life, they are always believing that they need to gain control. Sometimes they will do things not because it is right or wrong, but simply because they want to do it. Being controlled, nothing else. Their need is always focused on importance and growth. They want to feel special all the time. In a group of ten people, you will see, the shark will always talk more. Why? Because the shark wants to show "I am there, I am important. Is there something wrong with being a shark? No, but should I use the shark style all the time? No, but should I use a shark style sometimes? Yes, of course. You need the shark style. When do you need the shark style? What is the best time to use a shark? When you're in board meetings or in your personal life or in your official life, where you achieve goals, you ask yourself a question- "What is more important? a Goal or a relationship?" In this situation, you'll observe that the goal is more important than the relationship. That can be in th e office and also that can be at home.

For example- your son is not studying or your daughter is not studying. And now the exam is after tomorrow. At this point in time, what is more critical for you? Your relationship with your son or the goal of helping the son study and get good marks? If you become too sweet to your son or daughter, you say "Study when you want". If you become relationship-oriented. What person here, it will not work right now. So you become a shark here and scold your children to study. You always need to ask yourself the question- "What is more important, the goal or the relationship?" When you find the answer, that goal is more important than the relationship; you have a sacrifice going up. Which side will you use? Now you use the shark side, which is Yang energy?

3. Teddy Bear

Now let's move to the third side **"Teddy Bear"**. This is everybody's favorite site. My favorite type too. If you must have seen a teddy bear. Am I asking you "How does the Teddy bear look?" Your answer would be Cute, Sweet, Lovely, and Cuddly. What is more important to the teddy bear's behavior? Relationships are more important. They are not highly ambitious. They're not very interested in goals. So which energy will you call this? Yin energy or Yang energy? Absolutely this is the Yin energy. They're not very interested in Yang. So you'll observe, they're a very submissive type of people. Their emotional pattern is- "caring". They are very, very caring people. Like even if they are hurt they still care for others. For example, you're walking on the road and there are two types of people, one is a shark, and the second is a teddy bear. One is Yang energy, the second is Yin energy. And they both are riding a bike. And by the state, you dash them both on the same bike. Both got hurt a little bit. The shark also got hurt and the teddy bear also got hurt. How will the shark react? With Anger and Aggressiveness, right? How will the teddy bear react? What will the teddy bear ask? Yeah, the teddy bear will say it's okay. In fact, the teddy bear will come and say, are you fine? So is it good to be a bear all the time? No. it's not. Because if you're Yin energy all the time then people take you for granted also. So what do you do? Sometimes you become a teddy bear, sometimes you become a shark. How do you decide? Do you become a teddy bear in your personal life or do you decide to become a teddy bear in your professional life? Can you imagine which category would work better in your personal life or which one will work in your professional life? In order to get your answer you have to ask yourself the question "What is more important? Goal or relationship? That can happen at work and at home also. Goals can be important at home as well as at work also. Similarly, relationships can be important at home as well as at work also? So ask yourself the question then you can decide.

Whether you want to use that belief. Is it good to sacrifice? Teddy bears believe- it's good to sacrifice their life. They need a lot of connections. They need a lot of love. They need a lot of connections. They need a lot of friends. They always need people around them. Their result is always lost. Well, they are always sacrifices because of which they try to lose. They make other people win. Is it good to lose? It's not good to lose every time but sometimes it's okay to lose. For Example, you're talking to your father, and your father is giving you some unnecessary advice- "Son you should come home on time", why do you come late? If you're a shark, what reply do you give? Your shark says it's my life papa, I will decide. I've grown up now. Don't give me so much advice. Sometimes you talk to your parents like the way you answer you're becoming a shark. What is more important here? Goal or relationship? With your father, what is more important? The goal of being right or your relationship with your father? What is more critical here right now? I think the relationship with the father is more important. So at this moment, what is better? Shark or Teddy? Yin or Yang? So what should you tell your father? Okay, papa! Your papa also knows you will come late and you also know you will come late. But the point is not that.

The point is to give your papa that is giving him that feeling of he's winning, you are losing important in this situation, and it's okay to lose. Sometimes it's good to sacrifice for relationships. Yes. Excellent.

4. Owl

Now, let's learn the last style. This is a style that has to be learned. Not everybody knows the style. The first three styles we automatically learn when we grow up. And one of these styles has become our strength. The last style is called **OWL**. The style is called assertive. The owl is someone who can say something negative in a positive way. That's called an assertive style. An owl is someone who can stand up for their point and say: no, I don't like this. An owl is somebody who can stand up for their point and say: I like this. Assertive means standing up for your point. Assertive means saying what you want but respectfully and in a nice way. We are not talking about the Indian owl but the American wise owl. They call it there is a reason why we've chosen the word owl. If you go in front of an owl, will the owl suddenly fly away? Never, he will stay there, it will just stare and it will wait and it will try to understand if is this really a threat or something else. The owl will not jump into a conclusion attack like a shark. The owl will not run away like a teddy bear. The owl will not completely move away like a turtle. The Owl will judge, and the owl will watch. That is why it's a very assertive style. The emotions are very calm, always very calm, always very relaxed, they don't jump to conclusions. They believe that conflicts are good in life. Owls don't run away from conflict. They like conflicts. They need to contribute to other people's lives. They feel that the purpose of my life is to contribute to other people's lives. Owls believe in a win-win result. Which means I also win and you also win. They are deep in their heart, they're very nice people, and they will find a way to make you feel good also and to win the goal also, but does it mean that an owl will never become a shark? No, it's not necessary. An Owl can become a Shark also because an owl is a combination of a turtle, shark, and teddy bear. It's the best of all things, so sometimes the owl will find a greater way of win-win but sometimes the owl will become a shark and they will consciously lose a relationship. I think there's nothing wrong with practically, we cannot become everybody's best friend, and we cannot be loved by everybody in the world, so sometimes it is okay to lose some relationships. Owls also understand that sometimes they don't need to win the goal; they also need to win the relationship.

Let me ask you a question now, where an owl fits perfectly? In Personal life or in professional life? In which area can you play a winning game? The answer will be "Both". In this moment what is more important- Goal or relationship? The goal is also important, the relationship is also important. There is nothing called more important here or less important here. Every situation in life is very, very different. Every moment of life is very different. Because you're dealing with so many people, you are dealing with so many varieties of situations.

You can never really say that a particular style is best. Every style is important. You need to ask yourself the question "What is more important? Goal or relationship?" and adopt the best style. If you keep asking this question, your maturity in choosing the right style will grow. You can make mistakes in choosing the styles sometimes, but with time you will master the styles. If you do this, will you become a very flexible person who will have the power of both the Yin and the Yang? You can achieve it with just 30 days of practice. If you start practicing today, you will see a big difference in your life in one week. You will see that you are becoming calm with those people who always used to make you angry. On a piece of paper write down the names of people with whom you will practice this right now, tonight. Where generally you're very hard with them, you're very angry with them, you're very aggressive with them. But maybe tonight you'll become soft, maybe tonight you'll become nice to them, maybe tonight you'll let them win. And even if they're wrong, tell them that you're right. Sometimes it's okay to be harsh to people, sometimes it's okay to be a shark. There may be many people in your life who are taking you for granted. You need to become a little strong with them; you need to start saying what you want to say in front of them. You can use an owl style in this case. But remember win-win requires two parties. If the other person is not willing to play win-win, then what do you do? You can choose another style immediately. You have to learn the shuffling of styles very quickly according to the situation. Don't work on understanding, work on frequency. This lesson is nothing but a frequency lesson. You have to keep practicing and practicing and practicing.

If you work on a problem right now, your question to me will be, sir, my husband is a shark. What should I do? Sir, my wife is a shark. What should I do? Work on these lessons. Ask yourself the question and adapt to the best style. If you use it every day, you'll get better.

	Turtle	Shark	Teddy	Owl
Style	Passive	Aggressive	Submissive	Assertive
Emotions	Fear	Anger	Caring	Calm
Beliefs	Conflicts are bad	I need to gain control	It's good to Sacrifice	Conflicts are good
Needs	Certainty	Imp/Growth	Love/Conn	Contribution
Results	Lose/Lose	Win/Lose	Lose/Win	Win/Win

· · · ● · ● · · ·

Chapter Five
BALANCING YIN-YANG ENERGY & PRACTICAL APPLICATION

"Yin and yang are two halves that together complete wholeness. They balance and harmonize each other." - John Bellemy

THE ART OF BALANCING YIN-YANG ENERGY

We have now learned how to balance our Yin Yang energy. Let's do a quick recap, if you don't do the recap, you can forget a lot of things. So, the first lesson we learned was about preparing for our basic Law Fraction lifestyle. Point number two was about making sure that you are upgrading your frequency. During the entire Advanced Action course all the time, make sure that you're only and only focusing on practicing and upgrading your frequency, not your understanding. So don't get involved in questions, get lost in questions, don't keep getting worried about your understanding and questions. Keep practicing whatever little you understand. After that, make sure that you surrender to the universe because the more you surrender to the universe, the more the universe will support you. So just use the magic.

And then after that, we learned about lesson number one, which is the emotional habit tracker. After that, we learned about the Advanced Attraction lifestyle. Keep remembering that again and again and again. After that, we learned about FTBA Integration, "I have my feelings, my thoughts, my beliefs, my actions are 100% aligned with my goals". Then we got into learning about powerful words and then we learned about values, priorities, importance, proof of which is the DMF, time, money, focus, and space. What are the kinds of values we are talking about? Real values and artificial values. When you have real values, good qualities come out and you have artificial values, bad qualities come out. So, work on your values.

Three steps to check it: To upgrade your values, Drop your borrowed values, affirm your new values and dedicate the money, focus, and space to new values. After that, we learned about the purpose of our life, the purpose of our life is only emotions. So which emotions am I talking about? We are talking about "I want to feel, I don't want to feel". Which means positive emotions and negative emotions. We looked for the sequence of these emotions, which means the priority of these emotions, and if there is any conflict between positive and negative emotions. After that, we looked at making easy conditions and difficult conditions, which means making our positive emotions have easy conditions, and negative emotions, have difficult conditions. After that, we learned about making it easy to feel positive, making it difficult to feel negative, and finally, making your goals big, but making your emotional conditions easy. Once we learned about this, then we got into the Yin-Yang energy lesson, or in the previous lesson where we learned about what is the impact of Yin Yang, we learned about yin energy, female energy, Yang energy, and male energy. We also learned about recognizing missing qualities. Then we learned about making affirmations for those specific qualities which are missing in us right now. And then after that, taking small actions every single day. I also showed you a very practical way of matching your Yin Yang energy in different situations of life, which is the turtle, shark, teddy bear, and owl.

· · · ● · ● · · ·

Chapter Six
Understanding 7-Energy Chakras

"Yin and yang teach us that life is a continuous flow of change, and balance is found in embracing the constant transformation."
- Shannon Kaiser

We have learned how we can balance our Yin-Yang energies. Whenever you're talking about balancing your Yin Yang energies, there is one more technique that is very critical, which is "balancing your seven chakras". Put your right hand on your heart, from here till above your head are Yin Energy chakras, and from here to bottom at your feet are Yang Energy chakras. Most of us have no idea what a big role our chakras play in our life. Most of us only understand chakras as a spiritual concept, as an energy concept. Most people who have knowledge of yoga can understand this. In this chapter, we will understand what is the correlation of YinYang energy with seven chakras. Once you activate these seven chakras, what advantages will you get? And if you don't activate, and if some of these chakras are deactivated, which of your Yin qualities will be suppressed? Which of your Yang energy qualities will be suppressed? We will learn that trick.

There are seven chakras which are inside our body, near our spinal cord, at the center. But the energy of these seven chakras goes beyond 10ft of our body. Literally beyond 10ft of our body. Each chakra represents a body part where it is located. If you meditate a lot, or if you activate all your seven chakras in the way you are going to learn today, it goes literally beyond 15ft to 20ft. For people who are very highly charismatic all their seven chakras are activated. That means their Yin Energy and Yang energy both are fully activated. Now, what does that mean? Let's learn one at a time.

1. Root Chakra

The first chakra is the bottom chakra of our body and is called the **root chakra**. And the color is red. That is why the red color is shown over there, the sound of this chakra is LAM, and we'll practice this right now. Whenever you say the word LAM, you feel a certain vibration in the lower part of your body. This is at the tailbone, at the beginning of your tailbone. This is the bottom-most part of your body, your core part. This is known as your root chakra. Now, whenever you talk about the root chakra, it's your foundation of emotions. You are responsible for the way you feel. You are the source of your emotions. Whenever this chakra is deactivated, a person will constantly feel responsible and stable or irresponsible and unstable. When this chakra is deactivated, you will feel insecure. Your confidence level will be low. You will feel very Insecure in life. Even though you may have a lot of money, if your roots are shaken up, you will not be able to work hard. Your frequency of confidence is going to be low. This is Yang Energy frequency and if this is missing, you cannot have confidence to work towards your goals. You will not be able to take action, and you will not be able to stand up for yourself and say what you want to say to people. So this is the chakra. There is a particular frequency of the root chakra. Scientifically, the number is 396 Hz. This is not important for you to practice advanced perfection, but I wanted to give you this information so you understand that this is very, very scientific. Now, where would you rate yourself on a level of one to ten? One is very low and ten is very high on root chakra. Which means how confident do you feel about yourself? But wait, don't only measure confidence but also measure how good are you at taking responsibility for your emotions. Do you feel hurt easily? Then your number would be low. Do you get angry easily? Then your number would be low. Can somebody come and insert you? And it doesn't matter to you at all? Like you're absolutely peaceful about it. In fact, maybe you can think positively about the other person. Only then you can rate yourself nine or ten. I hope you have rated yourself. There's one person who knows you the most. Who's that? You yourself. So be very honest with yourself. Don't give yourself an unnecessarily high number. Be very honest with yourself.

If your root chakra is deactivated, no matter how many affirmations you say, will you be able to attract your goals? No, why not? Because you need to take action to attract your goals. But what will happen to your action frequency if your root chakra is suppressed? It goes down. You will not be predicting action because this is Yang Energy. A deactivated root chakra will lead to arthritis because it is the foundation. Your bones are the foundation of your body. And it can cause lower back issues.

2. Sacral Chakra

Let's move to the second chakra which is the sacral chakra. The sound is V-A-M. The sacral chakra is just two inches below your navel. So take your right hand, and put it on your navel at the center of your stomach. Put two inches below and near your abdomen. That's where you will find your sacral chakra. The activating affirmations are "I accept change easily", "I love managing uncertainty", "I love having fun", "and I enjoy experiencing pleasure". The frequency is 417Hz. This is the chakra of desire. This is the chakra of emotion. So anybody whose sacral chakra is deactivated will neither be able to feel too positive, nor too negative. I'll give you an example. You may know some people if you give them something exciting and ask them how it was. They will only say it's okay. If you give them something very bad, they say it was okay. It was not so bad. So for everything they will say it's okay. This happens to people when their sacral chakra is very, very low. It also leads to health problems. When your sacral chakra is very low it will lead to abdomen problems. A lot of ladies will start having women's problems when the Sacral Chakra is down. If your sacral chakra is down, what will happen to your emotions? A lot of people go and go through depression. If your secret chakra is very down and not fully activated, you will not be able to have the desire to achieve something in your life, you will not have that ambition and that aggressiveness to achieve something in your life. You will not be able to have control over your emotions. If your Sacral Chakra is down, you will not have control. So then what will happen to your goals? What will happen to your affirmations? They will not work. You will keep feeling negative in life. So how do you activate it? We are going to learn. The color of the Sacral Chakra is orange. Rate yourself again on a level of one to ten, how much would you rate yourself on a level of one to ten on Sacral Chakra, is it low activated or high activated? Do you feel your emotions are in control? Or do you feel your emotions are out of control? Do you feel you can enjoy both pain and pleasure? Do you feel you can take risks in life? These ratings are just to know yourself better and find yourself a solution to getting better. People who have low activation of the Sacral Chakra cannot take risks because it is related to feeling risky in life. People who have highly activated Sacral Chakra are able to take risks in their life.

3. Solar Plexus

The third chakra is the Solar plexus. The solar plexus is yellow in color. Take your right hand and put it on your navel. This is exactly where your solar plexus chakra is. Your solar plexus chakra is related to your self-esteem. It is the center of your body, your immune system. If your self-esteem is down, if your immune system is down, what will go down? This is ego. Anybody whose self-esteem is low, their ego will go up. What is ego? False identity of yourself. You feel you have something more than what you actually have. Or you feel you have something less than what you think you have. That is low self-esteem. Affirmations to energize this chakra are: "I respect myself and I respect everyone else". The people who can't respect themselves cannot respect other people. I'll give you an example. Have you met some people who are very senior but still talk to you with a lot of humility, lot of respect? Have you met people like that? We call these people respectful people. It is because they respect not only themselves but everyone around them, they're full of respect. If they are full of respect, they don't easily get hurt because they don't need your respect. They are already full of respect for themselves. If your self-respectDon't gets hurt easily, you say, "Don't talk to me loudly. Don't talk to me like this. Why did you say this to me? You didn't invite me to your birthday party. I really thought you were my close friend." If you feel like this your solar energy needs to be activated right now. Now, rate yourself again on a level of one to ten again, how much would you rate your solar plexus energy chakra? If you easily get emotionally hurt, your self-respect gets impacted. You don't achieve a goal and you start feeling low about yourself, you start having doubts about yourself.

One day I was talking to somebody in a meeting. He said, he started a project and made it grow. After one or two months when something did not work he started failing, and he started having self-doubt. He asked me what he can do now. Think about it, is this a problem-related question or a frequency-related question? It was a problem-related question. He said what should he do about his business. I said, forget your business and work on your frequency. He worked on it and again made it to success. We are going to learn this frequency lesson of working on your solar plexus.

The root chakra, the sacral chakra, and the solar chakra are the Yang energy. The decision-making, desire, ambition, and growth all of that is related to root, sacral, and solar limits.

4. The Heart Chakra

Put your hand on your heart, this is your heart chakra; your heart chakra is a beautiful combination between your Yang energy and your Yin energy. It's kind of a bridge between both. If you start activating your heart chakra, it actually starts activating your Yang and Yin also. So that is why they say love is the most important emotion in the world. When somebody opens up their heart, their Yin energy and their Yang energy opens up. Everything is activated from both sides. That's why the heart chakra is very critical. The color of the heart chakra is Green. And the sound is YAM. The frequency of the chakra is 639 Hz. The affirmation is "I accept love"; "I give love easily". When the heart chakra is deactivated, the First problem is people don't receive love. When somebody says I love you, we start doubting. Or think that he just wants something from us. We start doubting people who appreciate us. We just start doubting people who love us. We start doubting people who show too much positive energy towards us. Sometimes we keep asking ourselves, do I really deserve this? If you get something for free, you get very scared. Is it true? If you get success, you suddenly start doubting your own success. This is due to your heart chakra being deactivated. People are coming to support you but you're not able to take the support. If people are coming to help you, you're not able to take the help. You will say: I don't want anybody's help. I will do everything on my own. You keep yourself alone, you are denying universal support. Why? Because your heart chakra is not activated. You don't only receive love but you don't also love others. If you activate this chakra, your personal life just goes to the next level. Now rate yourself again on the basis of the heart chakra. Ask yourself: How comfortable are you with compliments? How comfortable are you with receiving health? How comfortable are you giving love? How comfortable are you with the work? Find the answers in yourself and start activating the Heart Cha kra.

5. Throat Chakra

The next chakra is the throat chakra. The throat chakra is related to the sound of H-A-M, put your hand on your throat and start humming, and feel the vibration of your throat. If you repeat the sound it activates your throat chakra. The frequency of the chakra is 741 Hz. Affirmation of the chakra is: "I have the courage to speak honestly". People whose heart your throat chakra is deactivated, are not going to speak strongly, they don't have enough confidence in their voice. Even if some people have confidence in their voice, it can still deactivate throat chakra because they lie about it. Not because they're bad people but when their throat chakra is down they are always feeling scared to tell people. They feel if they tell people the truth people will feel bad about them and then people will take advantage of them and then somebody will try to manipulate them. If they have more money, people will try to take advantage of them. If your throat chakra is down you will not be able to say no. You'll find it very difficult to say no, you'll feel guilty to say no, and you'll feel bad to say no. You have stage fear and you're not able to make videos. Now rate yourself on a level of one to ten. My number here was two when I did this exercise for the first time, I used to lie a lot, and I used to be very scared of saying no to people. It was only later when I started working on these chakras; I was able to get that energy and that courage to say no to people and to tell people the truth without feeling bad about it.

6. Third Eye Chakra

The next chakra is the **third eye chakra**. If you want to feel it, take four fingers and rub it on your forehead just above your nose. It's very sensitive, if you touch your third eye like this you can feel that sensitivity, you can't actually keep doing this only for too long. This is a very vibrant energy. You can't tamper with that energy for too long. The third eye is related to trust. The sound of this chakra is OM and its frequency is 852 Hz. Affirmations of this are "I trust myself", and "I trust others easily". If you trust yourself, what kind of people will you attract? Trustworthy people. If you doubt yourself all the time, what kind of people will you attract? People whom you will doubt more and they will doubt you. This is related to your intuitions. If your trust in yourself is very high, you'll get a feeling and you trust your intuition. Now rate yourself on the level of one to ten. Ask yourself: How much do you trust yourself, how much do you trust others easily or do you doubt a lot? Are you very skeptical by nature? Are you very negative by nature? Find out the answers and focus on activating the chakra.

7. Crown Chakra

The next chakra is my favorite; it's called the crown chakra. The color is purple and the sound here is om. The sound for the third eye and the crown chakra is the same. The frequency of this chakra is 963 Hz. The affirmation is "I am God, We are all God ". When this chakra is low, people don't feel good about anything, they feel very lonely here, they feel disconnected from themselves, and they feel like they don't have enough support in their life. They keep looking for people who can support them. If you feel like this, do you know who you are disconnected with? That is your energy from the universal connection. And that universe is you yourself. So the idea of "I am God" and "we are all God", has to be activated. If you start believing you are God, you won't self-doubt, you won't be desperate. If somebody doesn't give you something and you believe you are God, will you hate them back for it? No. Will you manipulate people if you know that other people are God? No. People are very scared, even a thief is very scared to take money from a temple. Why? Because he believes he's taking money from God. But the same person is not scared to cheat somebody else because he doesn't believe they are God. But whatever we do to others comes back to us. We have already learned this. The basic contraction at the energy level, we are all one. Now again rate yourself on a level of one to ten, where do you rate yourself? Ask yourself: How much do you really feel spiritually connected to yourself? How much do you really feel like a God yourself? But the most important question is how much do you treat other people like God? Do you judge people a lot? Do you accept people easily? Do you see divine energy in everyone?

THE ART OF BALANCING YIN-YANG ENERGY

Summary of All 7-Chakras:

Chakra Symbol	Chakra Name	Chakra Sanskrit Name	Chakra Location	Chakra Color	Chakra Seed Sound	Chakra Element	Frequency (Hz)
	1 Root Chakra	Muladhara	Perineum	Red	LAM	Earth	963
	2 Sacral Chakra	Svadhishthana	Sacrum	Orange	VAM	Water	852
	3 Solar Plexus Chakra	Manipura	Solar Plexus	Yellow	RAM	Fire	741
	4 Heart Chakra	Anahata	Chest	Green	YAM	Air	639
	5 Throat Chakra	Vishuddha	Throat	Light Blue	HAM	Ether / Space	528
	6 Third Eye Chakra	Ajna	Forehead	Indigo	OM	Light	417
	7 Crown Chakra	Sahasrara	Top of head	Violet	OM	Thought	396

Now let's give yourself a total of all seven chakras. So if you take ten numbers, which is the highest number for each chakra? What is your total out of 70? If it is too low you should start working on these chakras immediately if it is near 70 you're doing good.

Now we will learn to activate your seven chakras. I will teach you two activities, and after these two activities, you will rate yourself again. And you will see the power itself.

The first activity is called sound meditation for activating all your seven chakras. And the second activity is called the seven Chakras energizers. When a chakra is already activated you also have to charge it more. For example, sometimes when a car battery is discharged, we have to give a jump start. That's like an activation. But is that enough? No. After that, you have to charge the battery also. You have to keep running the car for about 20 to 25 minutes. So the battery gets charged again. Only activating is not enough. So these are two exercises.

The first exercise is called the sound activation for seven chakras and the second exercise is about charging the chakra to their full potential.

• • • • • • • • • •

Chapter Seven

Sound Meditation for Chakra Activation

"The softest things in the world overcome the hardest things in the world." - Lao Tzu

Before you start activating any chakra, put your right hand on your heart, close your eyes, and relax your energy. If there is any tension on your forehead, make sure that you relax that tension. Relax your eyes. Let go of any tension on your shoulders. Relax your breathing. Now, take a deep breath.

Activating Root Chakra:

The sound is LAM. Take a deep breath. Start humming LAAAAAAAAAMMMMMM for about 10 seconds.

Activating Sacral Chakra:

The sound is VAM. Take a deep breath. Start humming VAAAAAAAAAMMMMMM for about 10 Seconds.

Activating your Solar Plexus:

Sound is RAM. Take a deep breath. Start humming RAAAAAAAAAMMMMMM for about 10 seconds.

Activating your Heart Chakra:

The sound is YAM. Take a deep breath. Start humming YAAAAAAMMMMMMM for about 10 seconds.

Activating your Throat Chakra:

The sound is HAM. Take a deep breath. Start humming HAAAAAAMMMMMMM for about 10 seconds.

Activating your Third Eye:

The sound is OM. Take a deep breath. Start humming OOOOMMMMMMMMMMMM for about 10 seconds.

Activating your Crown Chakra:

The sound is OM. Take a deep breath. Start humming OOOOMMMMMMMMMMMM for about 10 seconds.

Now keep your right hand at your root chakra and repeat- "I am responsible for everything I feel", "I am the source of my emotions". Take a deep breath and start humming LUM again for 10 seconds.

Take your hands just two inches up to your sacral chakra and repeat loudly: "I accept change easily", "I love managing uncertainty", "I love having fun", or "I enjoy experiencing pleasure". Take a deep breath and start humming VAM for 10 seconds.

Stick your right hand on your navel and repeat "I respect myself and I respect everyone else". Take a deep breath and start humming RAM for 10 seconds.

Keep your hands on your heart and repeat: "I accept love easily", "I give love easily" Take a deep breath and start humming YAM for 10 Seconds.

Keep your hands on your throat. Gently feel the energy and repeat: "I have the courage to speak honestly". Take a deep breath and start humming HAM for 10 seconds.

Keep your four fingers on your third eye. Feel the energy there and repeat: "I trust myself easily", "I trust others easily". Take a deep breath and start humming OM for 10 seconds.

Keep your right hand on your head. No need to touch your head. Just a little up. And repeat: "I am God ", "We are all God ". Gently touch your head, Take a deep breath, and start humming OM.

Put your hand down and just relax silently for a few seconds. Feel your energy. Slowly open your eyes. And as you open your eyes, just grab your hands together a little faster. Generate all that energy and put it all over your face.

You are done. I hope you are feeling Peaceful, relaxed, energetic, and fresh-hearted.

THE ART OF BALANCING YIN-YANG ENERGY

Now give yourself a quick number for your root chakra. How confident do you feel right now? Write it in your notebook. How confident do you feel about yourself? About your life that you are taken care of? How do you feel about your emotions right now? Write down on paper, it'll boost your confidence.

Now come to your sacral chakra. Do you think you can manage your emotions right now? Give yourself a number.

Check your solar plexus. How are you feeling about your self-respect right now? Do you feel you need somebody's respect right now? Give yourself a number.

Check your heart chakra, do you feel you can give love right now? Do you feel you can receive love right now? Do you think you can comfortably say I love you?

Check your throat chakra, and give yourself a number. Do you feel you can be honest with people right now? Or would you be scared to tell your truth?

Check your third eye. Do you feel like trusting yourself right now? Do you feel like trusting people who are in this community right now?

Now check your crown. How connected do you feel to the universe right now? How connected do you feel to everyone in this community right now? And when you say "I am God", how peaceful do you feel about it? How comfortable do you feel about saying I am God? You can realize that you are feeling very comfortable about saying "I'm God". Now say "Everyone is God", "I treat other people like God" and see how comfortable you feel about this right now. Give yourself a number. Especially, think of someone who you don't like, someone who troubles you in your life. Think of them and say "They are also God". Check how you feel. And give yourself a number for the crown.

When you have all the numbers, total all those numbers. Now compare your previous number and your new total, you must have increased for sure. You can see there is an instant raise. If you do this exercise every day for 30 days, imagine how you would feel after 30 days. Would that be amazing? Make a commitment to yourself that you will do it for 30 days. By giving just 5 minutes of your day you can completely change yourself. You can even do this twice or thrice a day. You can just sit peacefully in the garden and do this. You get up in the morning and you can do this first. Or you can do this before you sleep at night. Whenever you want, do it at least once and see how all your energy chakras get activated. Your Yin energy gets activated, your Yang energy gets activated and as a result of that, those qualities that you require to attract your frequency will also get attracted.

・・・●・●・・・

Chapter Eight
ENERGY CHARGING EXERCISE FOR 7-CHAKRAS

"The wisdom of yin and yang lies in recognizing that opposites are not separate entities, but rather two sides of the same coin." - Alan Watts

This exercise is called the energy chakra charging exercise. In the previous chapter, we learned how we can activate our chakras using sound meditation and in this chapter, we will learn how we can energize those chakras to receive the maximum benefit to transform our life. This is an exercise that has been used for generations and generations for many years. In Chinese medicine, even in Indian mythology, it has been used a lot. And this is the exercise that can literally cure cancer. All health problems are nothing but sickness within your body. But what is our body made of? Its energy. Every cell of our body is made of energy. When the charge of energy goes down, sickness starts developing in the body. For example, when you buy a new car, it works in perfect condition but as the car gets used over a period of time, then you start realizing small problems in the car. Why? Because the energy of the car is going down, the same happens with our body. It's been scientifically proven now that our body has these seven chakras. And if you activate these chakras, our chakras have the power to heal us and make us feel absolutely fresh and healthy. For example, you may have heard during the earlier times, at the time of Ramayana, Mahabharat, or the Bible times, people used to live for 100, 200, 300, or 500 years. They used to practice this exercise. If you start doing this every single day for about five minutes, you start activating all your chakras. But most importantly, you start charging all your chakras. Because you charge your chakras, any illness within your body starts getting healed on its own. Your immune system heals you.

So get ready to learn this. Stand up, you can start some music. Start with keeping both hands at your navel one over another. Both hands shouldn't touch, there should be a gap between both hands and also don't touch your navel. As you keep your hand there, take a deep breath and imagine that there's some energy in the center of your body at your solar plexus. Like white light energy. Every deep breath that you take, is expanding and expanding and expanding. So take one more deep breath right now. Now take both your hands and wave them horizontally in front of your navel, remember not to touch them. Bring them close and take them away again and again. You're generating energy like this. Keep generating it for a couple of seconds. Now go a little fast, slowly increase the speed.

Now take both your hands in front of your navel, this time your palms should face upward, now slowly move your hand exactly in this position upwards toward your head, and let them go above your head, all the way towards your crown chakra. When you reach above your head, flip the palms, this time palms should face downwards, start moving both hands down with palms facing down, and let them go below your navel, all the way down towards your root chakras. Now again flip the palms upwards and start moving your hands upwards, repeat the process,

After a couple of repeats, stop at the solar plexus again. Now keep the left hand facing up, and the right hand facing down, and move both hands in opposite directions. So the hand that is going down is facing downwards and the hand that is going up is facing upwards.

After a couple of repeats stop at your solar plexus again, keep your hand a little far away, and move them like you are holding an energy ball. Generate that energy. Feel the energy in your hands. Charge it one more time, and Generate that ball again. That white light energy ball (you may have seen in superhero movies or anime), Hold it, take it all the way towards your **crown chakra** and charge it by saying, "I am God ", "We are all God ".

Now bring your hands down and once again, let's start the recharging, go down, go up, move down. From your solar plexus to all the up your crown chakra and again all the way down to your root chakra, with both your hands. Now go one hand down, one hand up. Now stop at the center. Generate that energy again. Generate all that energy together. Come close and go away. Now generate that energy ball. You'll feel the energy more now. Take it towards your **third eye**, just keep it there, don't touch your forehead, and say, "I trust myself", "I trust others". Slowly bring your hand down.

Now go faster One down, all the way up, and then down, all the way up. Stop at the center. One hand down, one hand up. Stop at the center. Let's create that energy again. Get that energy ball. You feel it even more. Hold it. Take it to your **throat chakra** and say, "I speak my truth courageously".

Take your hands down, all the way towards your root chakras, all the way up again. Stop at the center. One hand down, one hand up. Stop at the center. Let's take that energy. Generate it again. Feel as if you're creating a wave of energy, Create that energy ball. Take it to your **heart** and say, "I give love easily". "I receive love easily".

Take your hands down, all the way towards your root chakras, all the way up again. Stop at the center. One hand down, one hand up. Stop at the center. Let's take that

THE ART OF BALANCING YIN-YANG ENERGY

energy. Generate it again. Feel as if you're creating a wave of energy, Create that energy ball. Take it to your **solar plexus**. Charge it. Feel that energy there and say, "I respect myself". "I respect everyone else".

Take your hands down, all the way towards your root chakras, all the way up again. Stop at the center. One hand down, one hand up. Stop at the center. Let's take that energy. Generate it again. Feel as if you're creating a wave of energy, Create that energy ball. Put it on your **sacral chakra**. Two inches below the navel. Put your hands there and say, "I can handle pain and pleasure both".

Take your hands down, all the way towards your root chakras, all the way up again. Stop at the center. One hand down, one hand up. Stop at the center. Let's take that energy. Generate it again. Feel as if you're creating a wave of energy, Create that energy ball. Charge your **root chakra**. Now take it all the way down. Towards the lowest part and say, "I am responsible for the way I feel"; "I am the source of all my emotions".

One last time, take your hands down, all the way towards your root chakras, all the way up again. Stop at the center. One hand down, one hand up. Stop at the center. Let's take that energy. Generate it again. Feel as if you're creating a wave of energy, Create that energy ball. Take it all the way up to your **crown chakra, Third eye, Throat, Chakra, Heart Chakra, Solar plexus, and sacral root chakra**.

Bring your hand up. Hold in the Namaste position. Close your eyes and just relax for a few seconds. Slowly open your eyes as you do that one more time. Rub your hands together, a little faster. Drop that energy all over your face. You can take a seat now. You must be feeling Pleased, Relaxed, Sweating, Dizzy, and Peaceful, Some people may have tears, Divine, Connected.

It is normal, sometimes you'll feel dizzy, sometimes you'll feel energized, sometimes you'll feel like crying, sometimes you feel extremely connected. But every time, this experience will go better and better and better. You may be feeling something you have never experienced before, it would be difficult to explain in words. If you felt like this for 30 days, 60 days, 90 days, six months, and One year, Will success and failure affect you anymore? Will life and death affect you anymore? Will people leaving you affect you anymore? Will anything discharge your battery? The answer to all questions is a huge "NO". In fact, will you be giving energy to other people now? Yes. So a lot of people ask me, "Sooraj, how do you have so much energy?" This is what I do every day. That is how I have so much energy. Because I'm constantly working on energizing myself. And where is this energy coming from? It's within you. There's an unlimited source of energy inside us. The electricity of your house can go away but this electricity inside you is unlimited. There's an abundance of this. You never have to worry about this. You always have unlimited energy. Do this every day and then see what happens in your life on a daily basis. In one week some crazy magic will happen in your life. First, you'll feel the magic inside and then you will see the magic outside. Because when you start feeling the magic inside, it starts creating vibrations and these vibrations go out and they start creating manifestations. And then one day you will see the magic happening in front of you. And here is the weird part; you will not feel as excited as you thought you will when you achieve that. Do you know why? Because you are not feeling incomplete now, you have fulfilled all your needs and you are perfect now. You will achieve your goals now but the beautiful part is when you achieve your goals, you'll feel grateful, not excited. You'll not feel like it is an out-of-the-world experience, you will feel it like normal. Will God feel weird about creating a miracle? Will God feel wow! Did I create a miracle? No. That's how you will feel when you have a miracle.

Don't you like to feel that every day? So start doing this today and start transforming into the best version of yourself.

• • • • • • • • • •

Chapter Nine
SHIVA: THE MASCULINE & FEMININE ENERGY TOGETHER

"In the dance of yin and yang, neither side is superior or inferior. They simply exist and flow together in perfect harmony." - Unknown

The Story of Brighu:

Brighu became so intensely devout about Shiva that he became very feminine. So Parvati felt a little irked by this. So he asked her to move. So Shiva was just amused by this tiff that is going on between his wife and his devotee. If you're not aware of this already, Shiva, in yoga, is seen not as a God but as the Adi Yogi, which means he is the first yogi, and the Adi Guru, which means the first guru. And today yoga as a science, yoga as a system, yoga as a technology for inner well-being is available to us only because of the feminine play that Parvati compelled him to teach. By himself, he would have never done that. So because he became the first guru, naturally he developed disciples and devotees.

Of the first seven disciples that he taught yoga to they are known as 'Saptarishis.' Of these Saptarishis, the whole of southern mysticism has come from Agastya Muni; he is everything to us here because everything that we know is from him. He was Shiva's direct disciple. Another disciple was **Brighu**. Brighu became intensely devout to Shiva, and he became very feminine because devotion is feminine. He became a great devotee of Shiva. So every day he comes and he wants to do... three times he wants to circumambulate Shiva, which means, he wants to do pradakshina three times. He doesn't start his day without doing that. And Parvati is right here. By now, she is also a fully enlightened being, but he ignores her completely and he goes only around Shiva, never around both of them. So Parvati felt a little irked by this. So, one day, she sat close to him. Then Brighu came and there was no way to go around Shiva without going around Parvati, so he asked her to move. This is the way of a devotee. They are not logical people, very feminine, but they are intense.

Parvati said, "Why should I move?"

He said, "I will go only around the Lord, not you."

Brighu saw there was not enough space for him to go around Shiva alone, so he converted himself into a mouse. So Shiva was just amused by this tiff that is going on and went around Shiva alone ignoring Parvati or excluding Parvati from the circumambulation.

So he looked at the whole thing and he grabbed Parvati and put her on his lap, just to see what he will do, how is going to circumambulate Shiva without circumambulating

Parvathi now because she is sitting on his lap? Then Brighu transformed himself into a bird and went around just Shiva. Then Shiva was completely amused by this devotion, very pleased and also amused by the way the devotee is expressing himself and the way Parvati is getting fired up, because of this discrimination.

So Shiva said, okay let's see what you will do and he just merged her into a part of himself. Shiva has become half Parvati, and half woman, half man.

This is half man, half woman. If one knows how to nurture this one to its fullest extent, this will become half-man half-woman and that is how it will be. So this is called Ardhanari, where he is half-man and half-woman. So he made her a part of himself, just to see what the devotee will do. Now Brighu made himself into a bee and went around only the right leg.

So, Shiva and Parvati, of them laughed and they said, "This is not a man, he is too feminine. What he is dedicated to is everything to him, he is blind to everything else." So he just buzzed around the right leg, refusing to go around the left leg, because this is Parvati. Then this childish way of devotion of Brighu was amusing and nice. But at the same time, Shiva did not want Brighu to be lost in his devotion and miss the ultimate nature of existence. So he got into the yogic posture of Siddhasana where there was no way for him to circumambulate his leg or any other part of his body. If he has to do it, he has to do it for both these principles of feminine and masculine. So this is how this body became like this, that it is half male and half female, or masculine and feminine in equal proportions.

If one knows how to nurture this one, both will be fully active and alive in every human being. If we let these two parts of us reverberate as intensely as the other, each one of us can be a 100% man and 100% woman within ourselves. The whole science of yoga is based on this, that you should not miss either the masculine or the feminine in you, because any of them will be a lop-sided life.

Now when we say yoga, we are talking about a dimension that is all-inclusive. It is not an exercise or a process for creating health. It is about the ultimate well-being of the human being in which you cannot exclude any aspect of life. It is about attaining a dimension beyond all dimensions. It is about a system and a method to use your own existing system as a ladder to the divine, to make your body, to make your mind, to make your emotion and your energies a ladder to the divine, to make yourself into a stepping stone towards your ultimate nature.

·· · ● · ● ● · ·

Chapter Ten
YIN-YANG AND TAOISM

"In the realm of yin and yang, nothing is ever purely black or white, good or bad. Everything holds a bit of its opposite." - Unknown

Tao is both dark and bright. It is both weak and strong, both soft and hard. It is open on all sides but contains within itself the yin and the yang. Taoism is about balance; it is about living in alignment with the Tao. Yin-yang is the principle of Taoism that exemplifies balance. It represents the coexistence of contradictory forces or elements within the universe, hot and cold, dark and light are a few examples of yin and yang manifestations. If we're able to grasp the deeper meaning of yin and yang and what it implies, it may put to rest a lot of existential problems we have in our lives, and my hope is that by the end of this chapter, you will understand the deeper meaning behind yin and yang and how it can enrich your life. Yin and yang are the opposite forces that attract and complement one another. Yin-yang is not to be confused with the Western concept of dualism because unlike dualism the two sides are not at war in yin-yang. The opposite forces of yin and yang fit together seamlessly and work in harmony. So what is the principle of yin yang and how can it help us live a more fulfilled life in these challenging contemporary times? The history of the yin-yang principle can be traced back to the 3rd century BC when it was popularized by the Chinese school of yin and yang. Which focused on philosophy and cosmology at the time.

While yin yang is a part of Taoism, the Chinese philosopher. Largely credited with this principle is zhu yan born in 305 BC zhu zooming held the belief that life passes according to five phases fire water metal wood and earth. These phases would continuously interchange according to the principle of yin and yang. The five phases are used to describe the transformation of nature as follows: wood represents the spring or a period of growth where vitality movement and wind are abundant, while fire represents summer a season of expansion with heat as characterized by the flowering of plants, metal is an autumn period marked by dryness harvesting and collecting, while water like the season of winter is a season of retreating marked by stillness contraction and coolness, earth is a transitional period associated with stability and dampness. The order of these seasons will change according to two tiny cycles of generating or creation and overcoming or destruction. In the generating or creation cycle, each phase gives rise to the next as follows: wood, fire, earth, metal, water, wood, and so on. During this cycle wood feeds fire. Fire creates earth which produces metals such as minerals which collect water that will finally nourish the wood, which means plants. In the overcoming or destruction cycle, each phase overcomes the other in a rock-paper-scissor pattern, water overcomes fire, fire overcomes metal and metal overcomes wood. In the washing, the earth is a transition state between wood and water, water, fire, metal, wood, earth, water, and so on. Nature consists of changing combinations of these five phases but they're always in balance. This means that yin and yang are not static; they have a balance that ebbs and flows which is why there is a flowing curve where they meet in the yin and yang image.

Nature is associated with both creation and destruction and yin yang follows this principle yin yang is the union of opposites often represented as the masculine and feminine energies that are part of life. It is important to note that yang and yin are not defined as male and female in terms of sex and gender, only in terms of energies each sex can be considered yin and yang based on context. In traditional Chinese philosophy yin and yang do not represent male or female, the book the fishing an ancient Chinese divination text often translated into Book of Changes, states that the phrase yin and yang was used to refer to light and dark. The significance of the names yin and yang as meaning bright and dark derived from the properties of the sun and moon. Yin represented as black in the modern image of yin yang is the feminine life force of receptivity, while yang represented as white is the masculine force of action. Yang is hot and dry while Yin is cold and wet. Yet both energies coexist in all life forms.

Yin Yang in Chinese Philosophy:

THE ART OF BALANCING YIN-YANG ENERGY

In traditional Chinese philosophy, the yin is represented by a white tiger while the yang is represented by a green dragon. The yin and yang forces are equal in their own way. The strength of the yin can be seen in its patience while the yang shows its strength in its capacity to know the right time to strike. Because the Yang dragon tends to be bold and fiery it has a tendency for chaos which is why it needs to be balanced by the tiger's yin energy characterized by patience and strategy. The yin tiger represents the metal element and the white color is characterized by purpose and patience with inner strength and transformative power, the yang dragon represents the element word and the black color is characterized by boldness and fierceness. According to the Chinese creation myth, yin-yang is a result of the interactions between two primordial opposing forces. Yin-yang emerged from chaos during the creation of the universe and exists in harmony at the center of the earth. Yin and yang achieved a sense of balance in the cosmic egg, leading to the birth of Pangu. The first human and the first gods. There is an ever-changing relationship between the energies creating the constant flux of the universe and life in general. Any significant imbalance between the yin and yang results in a catastrophe. We experience life as processes coming into being and passing out of being as being a non-being. Nature and hence life can only exist where there is yin and yang. Yang gives form to all things; without it, nothing can come into existence, and without Yin, nothing can pass out of existence. The yang originates from a shadowy outline which the yin fills up with a definite substance. Life is only possible when these two forces achieve a balance. When we speak of the yin and yang we mean the air or ether, collected in the great void. When we speak of the hard and soft we mean that ether has been collected and formed into substance, benefits, and righteousness have their origin in the great void, are seen in the ether substantiated, and move under the influence of conscious intelligence. Yin and yang energies combine to create life itself yin yang is a reflection of the Tao the ebb and flow of the primordial energy of Tao. Taoism encourages people to accept and live in this harmony based on yin and yang. To live in accordance with yin yang means accepting the constant dynamic motion of the universe. The intangible concept of being a non-being which keeps creation in balance. as shown by the quote below from the fishing "A primary matter of an ethereal nature now expanding and showing itself full of activity and power as yang now contracting and becoming weak and inactive as yin". If we pay attention and understand the yin-yang principle it can teach his optimism and resilience. Yin-yang shows us that everything has its opposite and everything is understood by contrast. What this means is that you know what hot is because you know what cold is. In Lao Tzu's book Tao de Jing, he writes that all in the world know the beauty of the beautiful and in doing this they have an idea of what ugliness is. This quote means that when we see some things as beautiful we understand others as ugly this inevitable contradiction is a way of life and if you understand it you can understand how to go through life and face the challenges that come your way knowing that is all part of the balance of Tao. We know happiness because we have known sorrow without one the other cannot exist or even make sense; this contrast of energies and experiences creates order in the universe. they create the flow of Tao to illustrate this lao tzu writes "Being before and being behind give the idea of one following another", order comes when we understand that opposing energies follow one another we learn to stop fighting the order of the universe and to take each step with grace, with this understanding yin yang gives us optimism and resilience to go through life knowing that each moment shall pass even if it's full of sorrow, for joy must follow for the balance to be achieved.

Yin-yang can also teach us to appreciate where we are in life and live in the moment. When Isaac Newton said for every action there is an equal and opposite reaction, he was referring to the laws of motion and physics but this also serves as another example of yin yang made manifest. Universal forces always come in pairs, equal and opposite. If the ground you walk on does not offer resistance in the form of friction you wouldn't be able to walk, you would slide, and if the platform you're standing on does not offer enough resistance it fails to support you and you fall. Imagine standing on a steady platform versus standing on a thin sheet of paper with no support in the middle. It wouldn't be able to resist the force of your weight. This may be a rudimentary extrapolation of yin and yang but it applies to everything in life. We appreciate life because we know death and while nature does not recognize life and non-life we do. We know that one day it will all end and so we try to make every moment count. We appreciate youth because we know one day old age will come. So we try and make our youthful moments count. The existence of these opposites gives rise to meaning and order. If we didn't know sorrow, happiness wouldn't carry as much meaning as it does. You wear warm clothes in winter because you know that cold comes with the season. In yin yang, each element helps us to understand and appreciate the other. Yin and yang can also teach us the importance of acceptance and balance in life. Yin-yang does not teach us to avoid one side of the force in favor of the other, instead, it teaches us to strike a balance with a little bit of both.

Looking at the image used to represent the yin-yang principle one can see that darkness equals light and there's a little bit of light in the dark and a little bit of dark in the light showing that there always exists some yang in yin and some yin and yang. With the concept of yin yang, Taoism does not advocate for extremes, instead, it calls for a delicate balance of both light and dark. There are changes and movements in several ways and therefore there are separate places for yin and yang and reciprocal uses of the hard and the soft. During winter you don't start living in an oven because it is hot and the outside is cold. Instead, you heat your room, find warm food and wear warm clothes. The goal here is to be warm, not hot, not cold but warm. A delicate balance is achieved between the inferno heat of the oven and the freezing cold of the winter, if one element offers more opposition than the other the balance is lost. We all love the spring but think of the droughts and floods when this delicate balance is lost. Yin-yang teaches us that the universe is composed of a subtle balance between various forces and elements. We are part of the universe, manifestations of itself and so we crave that same delicate balance within ourselves and within our lives. Yin-yang provides a harmonious and coordinated interplay of forces and elements within the universe. This harmonic existence comprises the flow of life and when you're aligned with it you start swimming with the current rather than against it. to live according to yin yang in your life remember this quote from Dao de Jing "When yin and yang energies join when hard and soft unite then substance is attained one yin one yang they need each other they work together know this Tao and you will be happy and strong you will live long and be beautiful".

• • • • • • • • • •

CONCLUSION

Congratulations!

You have come to the end of this book. A vast majority of the readers don't finish the book, but you did, so you deserve a pat on your back. I hope it was a good journey and hope you have a smile on your face as you are reading this final page of the book. After all, I was trying to build a Successful Destiny throughout this book.

I wish you a splendid life full of happiness and fulfillment.

Cheers,

Sooraj Achar

MAY I ASK YOU FOR A SMALL FAVOR?

At the outset, I want to give you a big thanks for taking out time to read this book. You could have chosen any other book, but you chose mine, and I totally appreciate this.

I hope you got at least a few actionable insights that will have a positive impact on your day-to-day life.

Can I ask for 30 seconds more of your time?

I would love it if you could leave a review about the book. Reviews may not matter to big-name authors; but they're a tremendous help for authors like me, who don't have much following. They help me to grow my readership by encouraging folks to take a chance on my books.

To put it straight, reviews are the lifeblood of any author.

"The Art of Balancing YIN-YANG Energy"

Please leave your review by clicking the above link or scanning the below **QR Code**. It will directly lead you to the book review page.

Or visit the "**Reviews Section**" of this book's page on Amazon.

It will just take less than a minute of your time, but will tremendously help me to reach out to more people, so please leave your review.

Thanks for your support of my work. And I would love to see your review.

• • • ● • ● • • • •

PREVIEW OF MY BEST SELLING BOOKS

Numerology Mastery Series

★ **Why do 80% of People Fail to Recognize their True Potential ??**

This **Self-Help** book will help you **Recognize, Transform and Navigate** your life toward a **Happier Destiny**.

I always say that your **Date of Birth** is so precious. God has placed many diamonds on your date of birth you are not aware of. It doesn't matter if your date of birth is good or bad. The idea is how you can take the best out of your date of birth. **Master Your DESTINY With Numerology** is a perfect, **complete beginner's guide** for those who are new to numerology.

★ What Role Does Numerology Play in Your Life?

- You have been surrounded by numbers since the day you were Born. Now use them to unlock your Destiny.

- Wherever you go in your life, the numbers always move on with you.

- When you are born, on the very first day of your life, you get your date of birth, which is made up of numbers.

- When you get admitted to school, you get your roll number.

- When you get your results, you get a percentage of numbers.

- When you get a job, you get a salary and EMP-ID number.

THE ART OF BALANCING YIN-YANG ENERGY

- When you buy any vehicle, it has a number plate.

- When you travel, you get a ticket and seat number

- When you check into a hotel, you get a room number.

- When you want to call a person, you have to dial numbers.

- When you get married, there is also a date attached to it.

- If there is Life, there are Numbers. You cannot get rid of Numbers.

★ Your **Name Spelling** also plays an important role according to your date of birth. Believe me or not, **30% to 40%** of your success or failure depends on your name spelling. If you keep your name spelling correct, you can achieve 30% to 40% more success in your life.

♥ **Master Your DESTINY With Numerology will help you...**

✓ Recognize Your Strengths and Weaknesses.

✓ Find Your Lucky Numbers and Colors.

✓ Correct Your Name Spelling without changing your documents.

✓ Choose the Right Profession.

✓ Find a Compatible Life-Partner.

✓ With Simple Remedies for All Your Problems.

✓ Check Your Foreign or Abroad Opportunities.

✓ Predict your Future Years, Months, and Days of importance, which helps you take Better Decisions.

✓ Understand the Behavioral Patterns of People Around You.

✓ Transform and Navigate your life for a Better Future.

★ If you are ready to make a commitment to yourself that you want to learn everything that is presented to you, then it is our commitment to you that this will surely help you a lot. There is no reason why this book will not change your destiny or transform your future. But, there is an important thing you must keep in mind, i.e., **"You will bring this**

change through TRANSFORMATION, not through MIRACLES".

★ If you learn **Numerology**, then

(a) "You will be **awakened**", which makes it likely to "**transform**" your life.

(b) Ultimately, "You will be able to **navigate** your life".

★ Life is all about "**Awakening**,", "**Transformation**," and eventually, "Knowing How To **Navigate** It?"

★ Order **Master Your DESTINY With Numerology** now to make the most of your **Health, Relationships, Career, and Money** by unlocking the **Power of Numbers**.

Check Out My Best Selling Books Here

Numerology Mastery Series

1. Master Your DESTINY With Numerology

2. Master Your NAME-SPELLING With Numerology

3. Master Your RELATIONSHIPS With Numerology

• • • • • • • • • •

Vastu Mastery Series

★ **How Can These Books Work Miracles in Your Life?**

This Self-Help Book is A Perfect Blueprint Describing Ancient Principles for Modern Living. A Step-by-step Practical Guide for Beginners to Creating a Positive Living Space and for Optimal Well-Being.

Learn:

★ **How to Implement Feng-Shui/Vastu in your Day-to-Day Life !!**

★ **What Role Do Feng-Shui and Vastu Play in Your Life?**

★ **Relationship between Vastu and Feng-Shui?**

Vastu is used to Diagnose, and Feng Shui is the Remedy. Vastu is used to identify the disease, and Feng Shui is the medicine. Vastu and Feng Shui are complementary to each other.

Vastu Shastra is an Ancient Indian Science of architecture and construction, which is based on the principles of harmony and balance between humans and their environment. The main focus of Vastu is to create a harmonious balance between the 5-Elements of nature, i.e., Earth, Water, Air, Fire, & Space. It emphasizes directions and orientation and uses various elements like colors, shapes, and materials to create a balance and positive energy in the living spaces.

Feng Shui, on the other hand, is a Chinese Philosophical System of harmonizing everyone with the surrounding environment. It is based on the principles of Qi (Chi), the life force that flows through all living things, and Yin and Yang, the balance of opposite forces. Feng Shui focuses on the placement of objects, furniture, and structures in living spaces to optimize the flow of energy, or "Qi." It also considers the orientation of the building, the placement of doors and windows, and the use of colors, shapes, & materials to create balance & harmony.

In summary, both Vastu and Feng Shui aim to create balance and harmony in living spaces, but Vastu is more focused on directions and orientation, while Feng Shui emphasizes the flow of energy & balance of opposing forces.

★ The Benefits of Reading This Book Include:

✓ **Health and Well-Being:** Vastu principles aim to create a harmonious and balanced environment that can promote physical, mental, and emotional well-being.

✓ **Financial Prosperity:** Vastu principles are believed to help attract positive energy and good fortune, leading to financial prosperity.

✓ **Improved Relationships:** Vastu principles can help create an atmosphere of peace and harmony, which can lead to improved relationships with family, friends, & colleagues.

✓ **Increased Productivity:** A Vastu-compliant environment is said to be conducive to productivity and efficiency, leading to greater success in personal & professional life.

✓ **Spiritual Growth:** Vastu principles are based on ancient Vedic knowledge and aim to promote spiritual growth & enlightenment.

✓ **Enhanced Creativity:** Vastu principles are believed to enhance creativity and inspiration, which can be beneficial for artists, writers, & other creative professionals.

✓ **Better Sleep Quality:** Vastu principles can help create a peaceful and relaxing environment, which can improve the quality of sleep and help reduce stress & anxiety.

✓ **Improved Mental Clarity:** A Vastu-compliant environment is said to help clear the mind and improve mental clarity, which can be beneficial for decision-making & problem-solving.

✓ **Enhanced Career Prospects:** Vastu principles can help align one's career goals with their personal strengths and abilities, leading to greater career success & satisfaction.

★ Overall, the benefits of Vastu can contribute to a more Balanced, Harmonious, & Fulfilling Life.

★ Order "Master Your DESTINY With Vastu" now to make the most of your Health, Relationships, Career, & Money by unlocking the Power of Directions.

Check Out My Best Selling Books Here

1. Master Your DESTINY With Vastu

2. Master Your GROWTH With Vastu

3. Master Your WEALTH With Vastu

4. Master Your CAREER With Vastu

Ultimate Self-Healing Mastery Series

"The Art of Balancing Yin-Yang Energy" is an enlightening and transformative guide that unveils the ancient wisdom of harmonizing the opposing forces of Yin and Yang within ourselves and the world around us. Drawing from the profound teachings of Eastern philosophy and modern-day practices, this book offers a comprehensive understanding of Yin and Yang and provides practical techniques to achieve balance, harmony, and fulfillment in all aspects of life.

In today's fast-paced and chaotic world, finding balance is more crucial than ever. Whether you seek to improve your relationships, enhance your well-being, or achieve success in your career, understanding and aligning the Yin-Yang energy within you can be a game-changer. This book takes you on a transformative journey, guiding you through the principles, practices, and benefits of embracing the art of balancing Yin-Yang energy.

By delving into the core concepts of Yin and Yang, you will gain insights into their dynamic interplay and learn how to identify and rectify imbalances in your life. Discover how the complementary forces of Yin and Yang manifest in various aspects, such as work-life balance, emotional well-being, and personal growth. With this knowledge, you can cultivate harmony and create a fulfilling and purpose-driven life.

★ Here are the <u>Top-15 Benefits</u>:

1. Harmony and Balance: Balancing yin-yang energy promotes a sense of harmony and balance within oneself and in relationships with others.

2. Enhanced Well-being: Balanced yin-yang energy contributes to overall physical, mental, and emotional well-being.

3. Stress Reduction: Maintaining balanced yin-yang energy helps reduce stress and promotes a state of calmness and relaxation.

4. Increased Energy: Balancing yin-yang energy enhances vitality and boosts energy levels.

5. Emotional Stability: Harmonizing yin-yang energy supports emotional stability, reducing mood swings and promoting emotional resilience.

6. Improved Focus and Clarity: Balanced yin-yang energy enhances mental clarity, concentration, and focus.

7. Better Decision-Making: When yin-yang energy is in equilibrium, it fosters better decision-making skills and promotes sound judgment.

8. Enhanced Intuition: Balancing yin-yang energy can amplify intuition and inner wisdom.

9. Improved Relationships: Harmonizing yin-yang energy cultivates healthier and more balanced relationships, promoting understanding and cooperation.

10. Greater Creativity: Balanced yin-yang energy can enhance creativity and innovation in various aspects of life.

11. Physical Healing: Balancing yin-yang energy supports the body's natural healing abilities and can contribute to faster recovery from illnesses or injuries.

12. Emotional Healing: Harmonizing yin-yang energy aids in emotional healing and facilitates the release of emotional blockages.

13. Enhanced Digestion: Balanced yin-yang energy promotes optimal digestion and helps alleviate digestive issues.

14. Hormonal Balance: Balancing yin-yang energy can help regulate hormonal imbalances and improve overall hormonal health.

15. Improved Sleep Quality: Harmonized yin-yang energy promotes better sleep quality and can help alleviate sleep disorders.

Check Out My Best Selling Books Here

1. The Art of Balancing YIN-YANG Energy

• • • • • • • •

TESTIMONIALS

These are a few feedbacks from my clients across different parts of the world. Kindly go through their reviews to understand how Numerology and Vastu helped them.

1. Ekta Gupta – Kolkata, India

"2021 is a difficult year for me. I have consulted a few numerologists. I have received vague answers and complicated solutions. I'm new to numerology. Charges were expensive. Sooraj is a good and kind soul. He is very patient with me. He answered all my questions. I had 1000 questions. More ever he helped me to find a business name with no extra charges. I'm grateful to him. With your help, I'm sorted

out with my business name. I had a lot of anxiety about it. I'm confident now. Sooraj is a helpful soul. He is patient and explains if one has questions. He doesn't rush into closing the job. You can consult him easily. I am going to recommend him to newbies like me. He is not going to cheat you or misguide you".

2. Neetu Ganglani - Stanley, Hongkong

"Hello Sooraj, I can't thank you enough. At the age of 45, I could find an ideal life partner for myself. And my compatibility with the boy I like. Got to know our strengths and weaknesses. Your suggestions helped me to find the right life partner. You have a bright future. Good luck"

3. Lensly Kwaimani - Solomon Islands, Oceania

"Dear friend, glad I came across you. My daughter Felinda Kwaimani is sick for a long

time and I was very much worried. Thank you for giving suggestions and guidance".

4. Seham Shabhir - Talagang, Pakistan

"You're one of the best numerologists...your predictions are correct...you are a very humble person...you gave answers to all of my questions in detail ... I'm very thankful to you. Ur remedies prove very helpful for me. He is the very best numerologist... I recommend him for all.. u should consult him to get rid of your problems..his remedies work like a magic"

5. Naveen Kumar - Bengaluru, India

"Sooraj is a gem as a human and as a professional. Before approaching Sooraj, I have enquired and got inputs from other numerologists and I did some research as well. I Was not satisfied with the answers provided by them and most of them were behind fees,

even after paying for the consultation they charge extra for clarifying doubts. However, Sooraj was awesome in client satisfaction and the way he follows up with the client for providing suggestions. He takes the initiative to follow up and provide the best solutions and describes the reason for the input. I definitely suggest Sooraj to anyone who is looking for start-up business names or anything related to numerology. He has a good amount of knowledge and patience to answer all my queries".

6. Sneha S - Karnataka, India

"Hi Sooraj, it's a great prediction starting from Personality Traits to our Abroad Opportunities to future achievements. Everything is perfectly predicted with correct proof and explanations which help us to understand our lives better and take steps accordingly to numerology. Everyone are curious to know more about their life just to know when, how & what situations

they will come across and how they need to overcome everything. Thanks a lot, Sooraj, for the best Numerology Prediction which helped us to understand ourselves better".

7. Aditya S - Mumbai, India

"Sooraj, your numerology predictions are brilliant and accurate. Your Suggestions helped me find out whether my current job is suitable for me or not. I would suggest people consult you in due course of time".

8. Nabanita M - West Bengal, India

"Hi Sooraj, it's helpful and gives me a quick idea and help. Thank you so much for being there. It helped me to understand my situation It helps in my career and marriage. The information is good".

9. Naresh – Bangalore, India

"Hello Sooraj, it was satisfactory. Can decide further based on the info shared & also can see positive outcomes looking forward to checking how it works".

10. Harishchandra Dnyaneshwar Deshmukh – Delhi, India

"Hi sir, Padhai puri nahi kar paya, 11 k salary he, Stable nahi hu life me, Business success nahi milta. Thank u sir for sharing my report and helping me understand my strengths and weaknesses".

· · · · • · • · · ·

AUTHOR PROFILE

 Follow **Author's Profile Page** to get updates on all his books: **https://amazon.com/author/sooraj_achar**

 Grab your **Free Gift** if you missed it: **https://gift.sooraj-achar.com/**

 Please Leave Your **Valuable Review** here: **Master Your DESTINY With Numerology**

 For 1-to-1 consultation, scan the **QR code** or contact: **connect@sooraj-achar.com**

 Follow the **Author's BookBub** Profile: **https://www.bookbub.com/authors/sooraj-achar**

Stay Connected to the below **Author's Social Media Handles**:

https://amzn.to/3CgQHF9

https://medium.com/@soorajachar99

https://bit.ly/3M7gIu2

instagram.com/psychology_of_numberz/

https://bit.ly/3dO6aDh

https://bit.ly/3LXBTyz

SOORAJ ACHAR

https://bit.ly/3E9vKxc

DISCLAIMER

This book is for educational purposes only. Readers acknowledge that the author does not render legal, financial, medical, or professional advice. The content within this book has been derived from various sources. Please consult a licensed professional before attempting any techniques outlined in this book.

By reading this document, the reader agrees that under no circumstances is the author responsible for any direct or indirect losses incurred as a result of the use of the information contained within this document, including but not limited to errors, omissions, or inaccuracies. Adherence to all applicable laws and regulations, including international, federal, state, and local governing professional licensing, business practices, advertising, and all other jurisdiction, is the sole responsibility of the purchaser or reader.

Neither the author nor the publisher assumes any responsibility or liability whatsoever on behalf of the purchaser or reader of these materials. Any perceived slight of any individual or organization is purely unintentional.

Could You Please Leave A Review On The Book?

One Last Time!

I'd love it if you could leave a review about the book. Reviews may not matter to big-name authors; but they're a tremendous help for authors like me, who don't have much following. They help me to grow my readership by encouraging folks to take a chance on my books.

To put it straight– reviews are the life-blood of any author.

Please leave your review by clicking the below link, it will directly lead you to the book review page.

It will just take less than a minute of yours, but will tremendously help me to reach out to more people, so please leave your review.

Thank you for supporting my work and I'd love to see your review of the book.

Made in the USA
Middletown, DE
01 October 2023